OUR UNITY
IS IN
THE KING OF KINGS

Molly Sutherland writes a wonderful book that will bring healing to your heart as you pursue unity with one another in His Church. I believe this book can be used as a major catalyst to bring down denominational walls and help fulfill Jesus' prayer in John 17, that we truly will be one as God is One.

Che Ahn
Senior Pastor
Harvest Rock Church
Pasadena, CA

Molly Sutherland has a heart for unity that clearly reflects the heart of God. In ten, easy to read chapters, she challenges her readers to consider the subject anew. Her concern for Christian unity is based solidly in the Scripture she clearly loves. Her experience in a range of Christian communities, from Catholic to Pentecostal, provides her with a range of insights that can help others who are challenged by denominational limits. Her arguments for pursuing and maintaining unity are clearly stated and well illustrated. Her appeal to all who read her book is simple. I would happily recommend this book for use in seminars, Sunday school lessons, and personal devotional life.

Cecil M Robeck, Jr
Professor of Church History and Ecumenics
Fuller Theological Seminary
Pasadena, CA

Thank you for sending me your book on *Unity*. It is good to have a book on a subject about which Jesus Christ prayed so fervently *that all may be one*. I hope many people will be able to read what you have written and so come to a fuller unity with each other and with Jesus Christ.

Cormac Murphy O'Conner
Archbishop of Westminster
London, England
(Catholic)

OUR UNITY
IS IN
THE KING OF KINGS

MOLLY SUTHERLAND

All Scripture quotations are from the Good News Bible (Today's English Version) with Deuterocanonicals/Apocrypha ©1966, 1976, and 1979 by the American Bible Society and the New Open Bible (New King James version) © 1990, 1985, and 1983 by Thomas Nelson Inc.

Throughout this manuscript except where indicated (NKJ), I have used the Good News Bible, because it was designed with a limited vocabulary so as to reach as many people as possible who speak English as a second or even a third language. The numbers in the text refer to the Scripture reference given at the end of each chapter.

Print information available on the last page.

Rev. date: 07/13/2015

To order additional copies of this book, contact:
Xlibris
800-056-3182
www.Xlibrispublishing.co.uk
Orders@Xlibrispublishing.co.uk
521424

CONTENTS

LIST OF GRAPHICS
AND ILLUSTRATIONS

DEDICATION

I would like to offer this book to God, who I believe is the real author. May He do whatever He wishes with it. Thank you, Lord, for Your wisdom and inspiration without which it could never have been written. Thank you for my life.

ACKNOWLEDGEMENTS

I would like to acknowledge all those who inspired and helped to get the format and content into readable order. I especially mention Christine Sutton, Shirley Castiglia, and Pam and Cris Tober for their tireless dedication to making sure the presentation was good; Sharon Edwards, who first read and corrected the script and encouraged me to print it; Michael Kaufman, who double-checked all Scripture references and was always available to fix problems and give support; Rod Bradley, for hours of help on computer instruction; Wolfgang Kovacek, who enabled me to present the graphics well and print the first version of this book electronically; Kay Myregard, my main graphic artist, who designed the cover and who has encouraged me greatly; David Yapp, who worked tirelessly on the original graphic art; Karen Bradley, for enabling graphic six to be added; the RLM team, for their prayer and devotion that sustained me; and Celeste Lewis, who made sure I was safe and fed!

I am also indebted to Diana Chapman for her book *Britain's Spiritual Inheritance*, which inspired me to write Chapter 6, (Unity with Our Past Heritage), and also to Dr M. Brown for his book *The REAL Kosher Jesus*, which helped me to write Chapter 10, and to Ursula Sutherland for her hours of editing and referencing the scriptures of both chapters.

A special thank you to my four children who always encourage me and are a wonderful blessing to me. I hope one day all my grandchildren will read this, but all in good time!

May God bless you all, especially all who read it!

FOREWORD

The original book, which was entitled *Unity* and was written and self-published in 2006, now contains two extra chapters, Chapter 6, Unity with Our Past Heritage, and Chapter 10, Unity of Heart Between Jews and Christians, one family under God.

In today's world, there is a real urgency for us to stand together and witness the love God has given us all to communicate across the world. Deception, greed, arrogance, and self-centredness are the opposite of how God has planned us to live, for they lead to despair, depression, and fear. I believe God is shaking His world to wake us up, for the ways we have been living are causing huge problems, which we are at a loss to solve. Since He designed this world, He alone knows how we are meant to be living so that peace, prosperity, order, and happiness are experienced individually and corporately. When we put God in His rightful place, then all else falls into place. If we take Him out of the equation, everything else gets corrupted. This we are seeing clearly in today's world.

There is a real need for us to make sure of our roots, which is why I have added these two chapters. If our roots are not firm, we can find standing much more difficult to do. But the need for Christians to stand strongly together and evidence God's love has never been greater.

Today, I received an email showing on YouTube the wonder that has just happened. What an amazing time we live in! Things are happening so fast; it is hard to keep up. The video I was sent shows clearly how God is bringing His fractured Church together. Bishop Tony Palmer (Anglican) was asked to address the huge Pentecostal conference of world leaders, hosted by Kenneth Copeland. Tony knew well both Pope Francis and Kenneth through whom he had found the Lord twenty years ago. On video, the Pope expressed unity with this conference as 'we are all brothers in the Lord'. It was a sincere message from his heart to theirs, and he ended by asking that they pray for him as he would for them. The whole conference prayed for him, and this was recorded and sent back to Pope Francis by video. Unity in Christ is the message of this book, and what a delight for me to get such confirmation that Unity is what God is bringing to happen in our time! What a God we serve! We are all His children, and He is calling us all to come home to Him. What a joy!

CHAPTER 1

Choosing Unity through Love

As a child, the disunity of Christians became painfully real to me. It set me on a lifelong quest for valid demonstrations of Church that Jesus would see as authentic expressions of the love He brought us from God, His Father.

I was born in India and raised in a Chapel environment in Wales. Preaching the Word and glorious hymn music that corporately raised us heavenwards were important. Through family circumstances, I came into direct contact with Catholicism (the story behind this is related later in this book). I spent my teenage years in a Catholic school, the only Protestant in the class. I was full of questions! We also had a staunch Anglican student staying with us, and she and I spent many hours debating the beliefs of various churches. While I loved the debating, I longed to know where I belonged.

Finally, one night, at the age of seventeen, I cried out to God with tears, 'Father God, which do you want me to be, Catholic or Protestant?' I left the decision in His hands, got into bed, and went to sleep. I woke up next morning, suddenly seeing why Catholics said what they did! I sought out a priest and asked him to instruct me. He told me who Jesus was and how He had died so that I could live in union with God. I fell deeply in love with a God who loved us all so much that He would send Jesus to bring us all back home to Him. After several months of tuition with this priest, I joined the Catholic Church.

Jesus drew me closer and closer to Him, and I wanted nothing more than to lay down my life for Him in love. He asked me to join an order of nuns whose worldwide work was among the very poor in the inner cities. I plunged deep into this life. There were nearly nine years from entering to taking one's final vows. It was a long and intensive training, and I loved it! Our day was divided into three parts: eight hours of sleep, eight hours of work, and eight hours of prayer. The first two years were deep spiritual training to ground us in practicing the presence of God in every situation. He lived in us, and unity with Him was essential to living the rigorous life of nursing impoverished people in their own homes who were sick. We never knew whom we would be sent to – a mother having her seventh child in dire poverty, an old bedridden lady so flea-infested that her neighbours could no longer cope, or a satanist lady who hated us but suffered us to nurse her as she was dying with a hideous breast cancer. We nursed anyone who could not afford to pay for help. We were trained to see in those we nursed the image of our Lord and to do to them as we would do to Him.

I loved the life to which God had called me, and I was surprised when midway in the sixth year it all changed. My heart was torn again – could God be behind this change? I only wanted to do His will, but was it His will or was this some temptation from the enemy? Could He really be asking me to leave the order? What was I going to do out there all alone? The Sisters had become my family. Those in authority over me in the order saw the tension I was under and suggested that I leave for a while to see what God was wanting for my life.

The Lord knows what is best for each of us. In His design, all of us have our own aspect of His work to which He has called us. I did leave the convent, but continued nursing in a London hospital. *What now, Lord?* I thought. He led me into marriage, where I learnt much that I could not have learnt in a convent, and we had four wonderful children! I learnt what it is to love a family of one's own and to be loved by them.

Then the Holy Spirit began changing His Church. The Charismatic Renewal swept across Britain and woke lots of us up to new and exciting possibilities. Christians joined together to worship Jesus, and I came alive. My husband recognised that this was necessary for me, but he could not have any part of it at that time. I could not understand why we were being divided. It was very painful, so to give him time, I stopped going to the meetings. I thought it was the loving thing to do, but he was furious that I had stopped, and he insisted that I should continue. 'You are coming to life, and I will not be responsible for stopping it. However, I must find my own way,' he said. We had been married twenty-four years when he left and remarried.

Again my heart was torn. Could God be behind all this? He was! He gave me early retirement from the Catholic school of which I was principal and opened the door for me to train in an evangelical Spirit-led college. This was confirmed as a *call* on my life by the three Catholic priests who knew me best. Their confirmations gave me confidence to follow God's lead to leave for a while what was familiar to me, the Catholic world, and to explore the Protestant one. Then, God clearly asked me to leave England and to come to America to a multidenominational seminary for three years to learn the Protestant theological languages. I came to study another side of Christianity and to taste many of the differences that exist in His Church. Following God can be a roller-coaster ride!

I was at the seminary when all sorts of people started to come to me for inner healing from past wounds sustained from life's struggles, and to my surprise, God healed them! I joined a ministry team led by anthropologist, Dr Charles Kraft. We went on mission trips to places like Morocco to encourage missionaries who were isolated from each other, lonely, and even depressed at seeing so little fruit for their labours. We also went to churches in Nigeria, Canada, and America. All the time, I was learning the ways of the different Protestant churches while keeping in touch with my Catholic roots. I saw the love for the Lord Jesus that they all had, amidst the fractured state of the Body of Christ. My heart went out to them all.

3

Wherever I went, I saw God healing His people. Soon, some of them settled around me and asked that I teach them how to work with the Lord to see Him heal hurting people too. This is how Resurrected Life Ministries was born. It is now a non-profit organisation dedicated to healing, training, discipling, and sending out others to do the same work.

To my delight, a charismatic Catholic priest asked me to come and teach in his parish. It thrilled me to be back again among Catholics! I have a foot in both worlds, for I have been trained by both. All these experiences have culminated in me the urge to write this book, which I offer to you. I feel it is the timing of God.

I love all denominations, for each has much to offer the others. Yet the world out there, to which we are sent, is confused by the way we treat one another. We often wound others and frame our beliefs in language we cannot communicate to each other without causing misunderstanding and further fracture.

We all need the Lord to unite and heal us so that we may act in unity and love, to bring His message of love to those He is calling to Himself. Jesus prayed, *Father! May they be one, as You are in Me and I am in you. May they be one, so that the world will believe that you sent me* (John 17: 21). I trust that this book will help us change our attitudes towards one another and thus prepare the way for the Holy Spirit to unite His Church as a powerful force against the evils we see around us. He is calling all Christians to stand together in unity. Will we obey His call or will we continue to criticise each other from behind closed mental doors?

Graphic 1 - Bird of Prejudice in Cage

Prejudice, Judgement,Unbelief
Spiritual complacency

CHAPTER 2

The Purpose of Unity

Last week, I was at an early morning prayer meeting where there were representatives from several different churches. One pastor started to pray earnestly. There were tears in his eyes that rolled down his cheeks as he shared with us the reason for his pain.

'Recently', he said, 'I went to the shopping mall to offer the Good News to some of the people there, but I had to stop. I tried three times with three different people. I tried to explain my purpose, but they each cut me short with the following statements:

'"When you Christians can get your act together, then come back to me!" (And he walked away.)

'"You are divided even from each other, why should I want to join that!" (They looked scornfully at me and turned on their heels.)

'"You can't even agree with each other so how can you teach me?" 'The people did not want to listen. I realised that our actions as Christians speak louder than any words I could offer. These people spoke truth, and it cut me to the heart. I haven't been able to get it out of my mind.'

This is the testimony of Christianity that the world sees. It sees us in division, competition, and self-centred interest, proselytising and criticising one another. Sometimes, we will not even talk to each other, but we backstab, and in some parts of the world, we even kill each other. *Why should anyone want to join that?* We are like many squabbling children, each trying to be heard over the others. *That is not what Jesus called us to be.* That is not what He taught his disciples, nor later what they went out to the nations to give. Yet it is the sad, sorry state of the Church today. We are a very poor advertisement for Christ. Often people will receive Christ. Unfortunately, it is the Church that later gives them indigestion!

Is it a hopeless situation? Fortunately not! Left to ourselves it would be. However, it will be God, Himself, that brings about our unity. *If the LORD does not build the house, the work of the builders is useless; if the LORD does not protect the city, it does no good for the sentries to stand guard* (Ps. 127: 1). It will be the Lord who unifies His Church. Perhaps the very escalation of evil around us will enable us to see the great need to come together to take a stand against it.

Each of the three people in our opening story was saying the same thing. If we Christians would 'get our act together', if we would show them our unity together, then they might listen. If our message would be demonstrated by the way we treat each other, then they might be prepared to hear that our way works! The world is saying, 'You change. Then come and talk to me!'

What would happen if the Church of today came to God and even to the world and asked forgiveness for the ways we have treated each other and them? What would happen if we begged God to change us, to unite us in His love and send us out together to demonstrate His love? If we cling to old resentments, old barriers, old judgements, and old negative stories about each other which we repeat, thus causing division, we are resisting what God desires to do. To resist God is dangerous.

So what is our attitude towards other Christians? We are not asked to agree with them; we are asked to love them. Can we do that from the safety of our own fortified denominational walls? I think not. However, we can make a beginning; we can repent to God for blocking unity through our prejudice and ignorance. We can ask Him to set up encounters with those from other Christian folds. We can invite them to a meal or arrange a time to dine out together and then listen to their hearts as they speak. This

7

could be a good way to start. Let us not go with the motivation of putting them straight! *Let us go to listen, respect, and begin to love people very different from ourselves.* Above all, let us notice how they live and let us observe their attitudes towards each other. They can often teach us a great deal about living and about loving, which, after all, is the way we put Christianity into practice. Let us forgive the negative we see and concentrate on what they show us that is wholesome and good.

What is our attitude towards the people around us? This is what people outside the Church look at. Do we treat people the same as they do? If so, *we are not taking the lead as we are expected to do.* Are we criticising, judging, arguing, and exhibiting anger and distrust of each other? Do we grumble and grouse about them? Do we talk about them when their backs are turned? Do we gossip about their problems? Jesus did not do these things!

What is the evidence that we are Christians? Jesus loves everyone equally. Are we giving this love to everyone equally? It is our integrity of heart that will cause people outside to take notice! People trust integrity intuitively. If they see that we are not behaving in a negative way, people will know they can trust us when their own backs are turned. Then they may more easily listen to what motivates us, namely the wonderful love by which we are all loved.

When my husband left, I was lonely and on occasion would go to a little group of Christians led by a Baptist minister on a Sunday evening. They were a warm fellowship, and I needed that warmth at that time. I learnt two things from them. *First*, I saw how the Holy Spirit was truly working with His Church. The very message that had been preached at the Catholic Mass from a set liturgy that morning was also chosen to be the topic used by this minister that very night! I saw the unity of focus on which the Spirit was directing His Church to meditate.

Second, I learnt an important ministering gift which I have subsequently always used, namely to look for God's image in everyone. The minister asked us to sing together many times as we walked around the church standing in front of different people and looking into their eyes as we sang the words, 'I see in you the image of my King and I love you with the love of my Lord.'

This I found quite daunting to do at first, but it has become a focus that I practise when speaking to people, especially those who come for ministry. People are God's creation, and no matter what sin-resulting distortions the enemy has laid upon them or what bondages they have fallen into, they were originally made in God's own image. It is essential that we learn to jump over the hurdles of the distortions and find the essence of the person hidden within. God chose to make us because He loves us, and we must learn to love in the same way. Isaiah records God as saying:

> *When you pray, I will answer you. When you call to me, I will respond. If you put an end to oppression, to every gesture of contempt, and to every evil word; if you give food to the hungry and satisfy those who are in need, then the darkness around you will turn to the brightness of noon. And I will always guide you and satisfy you with good things. I will keep you strong and well. You will be like a garden that has plenty of water, like a spring of water that never goes dry. Your people will rebuild what has long been in ruins, building again on the old foundations. You will be known as the people who rebuilt the walls, who restored the ruined houses (Isa. 58: 9–12).*

Jesus has told us to love each other. He even said that the way we love each other will cause others to know that He, our leader, really did come from God.[1] Wow! If that isn't a reason to concentrate on loving one another, then I don't know what is! So, loving each other is the greatest evangelistic tool we have. This is what catches the world's attention. As we lay down our lives for each other, the world sees something that stops them in their tracks. It is the opposite of the self-centred spirit that pervades the world today.

Many examples of this love came out of the Nazi prisoner of war camps. One such example was of a celibate priest who volunteered his life in place of a married man and walked into the gas chamber so that this man might have a chance of being

---

[1] I pray that they may all be one. Father! May they be in us, just as you are in me and I am in you. May they be one, so that the world will believe that you sent me (John 17: 21).

reunited with his family.[2] We may not be called to such heroism, but we are called to cleanse our minds and hearts of deep-seated prejudice against each other and to pray for and love people as Jesus did and does. We need to be on our guard to reject every negative thought that comes to us against another person. Then, if we do this, we can be sure nothing negative will come out of our mouths to destroy, rather than build up people in love. It all starts in our minds. *Loving thoughts lead to loving actions.* This has nothing to do with sentiment or even feelings of love. It starts to grow in our hearts when we bless every house or church that we pass in our neighbourhood, when we pray for pastors, priests, and leaders all over the world, and when we watch our minds and clamp our lips and smile warm smiles with our eyes. Love is the decision to love.

Graphic 2

The Eye of Love

It is not *our* love we need to give, but it is *Jesus'* love flowing through us to others. His love will unite us. It is His love by which

---

[2] The greatest love you can have for your friends is to give your life for them (John 15: 13).

we love. It is a supernatural spiritual love, not a fickle natural love by which we love others. *And how do we get such love?* Jesus said, *Ask and you will receive.*[3] As we receive, we give. The source of His love is never-ending. So the more we get, the more we can give out continuously.

But to go back to our opening story, why did those people walk away? What does the world want to see that will cause it to stop and listen and not walk away in disgust? They want to see us *evidence the love of God like Jesus did*. Then they will flock to listen and see for themselves. People were the same in Jesus' time as we are now. The Church (synagogue) of that day had so many rules and regulations that no one was able to do it all. All it produced were self-centred, hypocritical, arrogant people, who looked down on others and took the best of everything for themselves. Most *ordinary* people were working long and hard for very little and desperately trying to make ends meet. They were often sick from overload and anxious about many things that were beyond their control. They were very much like many people are today. God had promised them a Messiah, someone who would lead them to freedom from the tyranny and bondage under which they were forced to live. But He had been long in coming, and many had lost even that hope.

Then He came!

He did not look like what they had expected. He just poured out God's love everywhere He went. He lifted people so they could see life through God, His Father's eyes. He healed and enabled them to see, hear, dance, laugh, and feel valuable. They flocked to Him from all over His country, often walking miles with little food and nowhere to sleep. Such popularity challenged those in authority, and they schemed until they got Rome's permission to kill Him. (Perhaps you saw the movie, *The Passion of the Christ*, by Mel Gibson.) The death of Jesus was God's solution. Jesus stood in our shoes before God and took the hurt and the anger that God felt when we rejected Him. Jesus took God's pain and our rebellion and indifference into Himself. *On that cross, He became the*

---

[3] Ask, and you will receive; seek, and you will find; knock, and the door will be opened to you (Matt. 7: 7).

bridge between us and God, for He wiped out all that could separate us, so we could come to God freely and learn His way of love. From that time to this day, God is calling all people to come to Him: the old, the young, the sick, the healthy, the rich, the poor, every nation and tribe. He longs for us to come so that He can show us the secret wonder of life with Him. Life without Him makes no sense at all. We need to give Him the chance to prove His love for us. He will do this personally, for each of us is unique and special to Him. He knows just how to touch our hearts and change our lives. But He will not force us in any way. Coax, yes! Force, no! So why not talk to Him yourself? Tell Him honestly where you are at. Ask Him to show you His way, and He will, but be prepared for Him to do this in *His* way. Do not expect Him to do it in your way, or you may miss Him. We must let God be God!

If you are outside of the Church and are looking at it and shaking your head, thinking, 'When will they get it right?' pray for us and forgive us. Better still, come to Jesus, and together with Him, help us to change. The Church today needs to change to become a better witness for Jesus, our Lord. Do not stay away from Him because of us. Help us to change. We need you! The Church has so often failed to communicate His love, and you are right to show us that our division keeps you away. We need to ask your forgiveness for our self-centredness, our prideful stupidity, and our lack of love and unity. We are sorry that we have turned you off. We have been bad examples of God's love so often. However, one thing we know for sure is that God loves all people, and we want everyone to know this because it has changed our lives. He is changing us all the time to be more like Him. (As you have noticed, we still have quite a way to go, but it is happening!) He will change everyone who honestly wants more than what they have right now. If we all come to God, He will show us what life with Him can be like. 'Is it religion?' you may ask. No, it is a whole different dimension of life, not the natural life we know so well but a heavenly life, the very life that God lives Himself. Jesus came with a message. He said in modern language, 'You are living life the wrong way. It doesn't work that way. Turn away from the old ways and let Me show you a new way to live.' He called it being *born again*, born into the new life He came to bring. Only then can we see as God sees and begin to live His life of love. God wants to adopt us into His worldwide family. He wants to bless us with every heavenly blessing and show us how, through His Son, this new life is possible. He truly is the answer to our every need, and He is calling urgently for us to come to Him before it is too late.

'Come, let Me show you what life can be like. Come!'

Tell Him what your answer will be.

To illustrate the above, I have included two pictures.

The *first picture* illustrates the natural life we are all born into that gives us our natural identity.

Graphic 3 - First Birth

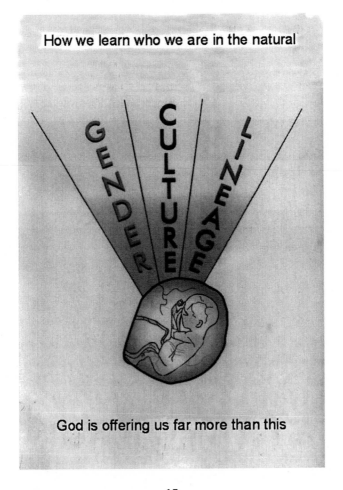

How we learn who we are in the natural

GENDER CULTURE LINEAGE

God is offering us far more than this

13

The *second picture* illustrates the new identity God has given us through Jesus. We are to live His values of love in His Kingdom and belong to His worldwide, multicultural family.

Graphic 4 - Second Birth

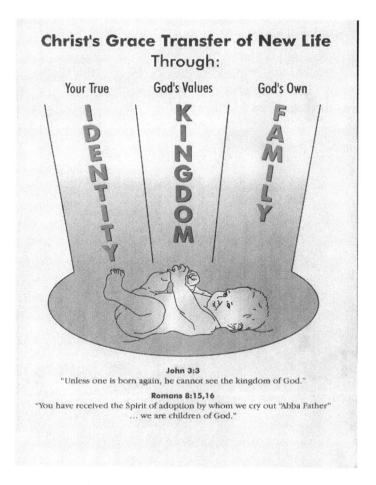

Christs Grace Transfer of New Life Through:

Your True   God's Values   God's Own

IDENTITY   **KINGDOM**   **FAMILY**

John 3:3
"Unless one is born again, he cannot see the kingdom of God."

Romans 8:15,16
"You have received the Spirit of adoption by whom we cry out "Abba Father" ... we are children of God."

We cannot live in both identities. God offers, but we choose! As we choose God's way, so He facilitates the transition from one to the other. The Holy Spirit, our guide to living in God's way, is continually enabling us to let go of our old way of seeing ourselves and life so that we may live in the way God first designed us to live. He is calling us to live His life with Him and to let go of our naturally oriented, selfish selves. He is calling us to unity with

Him. That's why He came to show us what this life looks like and how to live it.

For thirty years, He lived in His family, doing the ordinary job of a carpenter. *He showed us what the unity of family life could look like.* Then, God sent Him to the nation into which He had been born. Jesus was a Jew. He started to tell and show the Jewish people what God's love looked like. Those who responded were healed of sickness, delivered from evil bondages and wrong ways of living, and then were blessed with the new way of seeing in order to live God's way. He brought them into unity with Him and with each other. Then when they knew Him, He commissioned them to go to others and do as He had done to them. He even gave them the same Spirit He had within Him in order for them to do what He did. He called them His Church. He took ordinary, simple people and called them to live with Him for three years to learn how to spread God's love. He taught them by word and showed them by deed. Then He said, *now* go and do the same and I will be with you as you do.[4] *This is how Jesus sees His Church.* He has promised that streams of His living water will flow out of us to a very thirsty world as we do what He has told us to do.[5]

There are many people doing this all over the world. For example, Mother Teresa gave Jesus' love to the poor of Calcutta, and the world stopped with wonder. There are Heidi and Roland Baker who currently take in hundreds of unwanted children in Mozambique and show them they are loved and wanted by God. Clayton Golliher and his team of Hope for the Homeless Youth, who have been rescued themselves from the streets of Hollywood, go out to others who are lost as they had been only months before. There are many thousands at work all over the world, often hidden, and yet powerfully working with Jesus to bring God's love and new life to those around them. They are doing what

---

[4] Go, then, to all peoples everywhere and make them my disciples: baptize them in the name of the Father, the Son, and the Holy Spirit, and teach them to obey everything I have commanded you. And I will be with you always, to the end of the age (Matt. 28: 19–20).

[5] Whoever believes in me should drink. As the scripture says, Streams of life-giving water will pour out from his side (John 7: 38).

God has commissioned them to do. And it works! *But is there unity between these workers?* Do we know enough about each other to even pray for one another? There are communication systems now available whereby unity in outreach can be offered. Will we use them to bring focus and direction and even the pooling of resources or will we go on in our own denominational ways, even causing those we go to, to witness our divisions and have to choose between us? God raised Jesus to life again, and He will raise us, His Church, together with Him into unity. Can we look forward to this day? For in Him is the only real unity there is. He is with each of us wherever we go, so at this stage, let us at least offer prayer for each other and keep our focus on Him in order to help each other as He leads us. Let our love for each other rule in our hearts, and let respect and generosity towards each other rule in our minds. *Let us show people how we can love as He loves us. This is the unity He came to bring.*

In 1986, when I had just arrived at Fuller Seminary, I was asked if I would like to join a team going down to Mexico City to look at the poverty that was there and the difficulties people were having when they left their farms and came to the city to look for a better way of life. There was a conference going on there, and I was invited to attend. The conference demonstrated how two very different churches could join together to minister to the very poor living in cardboard shacks on the hillsides. The Catholic Church was represented by a larger-than-life Franciscan friar, who reminded me of Friar Tuck! A Baptist minister had been called by God from Northern California to leave his comfort zone and join with the friar. Both went together to those living in the shacks. They went to give God's love and to welcome them into His Church family. Their strategy was this. They would listen to the poor and, when possible, alleviate their current need (perhaps a corrugated tin roof to keep off the rain). As people talked to them, they would find out what their Christian family heritage had been. If it had been Catholic, the friar would take the lead. If their family had been Protestant or if they had no idea of Christianity, the Baptist pastor would respond. I had never before seen Catholics and Protestants working together to bring relief to people and to spread the Good News together in unity and harmony. *It can be done,* I thought!

Jesus listened to people. He saw their need, and He healed and restored people to life. He was totally dedicated to bringing God's love into their situations. He has asked us to decide to do the same and to join Him in this great work. What we decide will determine the type of life we choose to live. Mother Teresa and others have dedicated their whole lives to giving His love to the destitute, but it all developed in their minds as they made decision after decision to give out His love. We are all called to different types of society. The rich need His love as much as the poor. Whoever He has called us to live among need to see His love in us. Each decision we make to love leads to a greater measure of love being given to us to give.[6]

Every life is made up of millions of decisions. *It is those decisions that finally produce the person we will have chosen to be.* We are asked to love; it is the great commandment.[7] As we love, unity is spread, for love covers a multitude of sins; it nourishes and sustains, fortifies and builds.

Are we builders, sitters on the sidelines or part of the demolition squad? Let us be awake and aware for Jesus said, *Anyone who is not for me is really against me.*[8] His mission was to spread God's love, and He has commissioned us to go and do the same. Surely that is what a Christian is! We are His disciples, ambassadors of love to a dying world. Then for God's sake, let us show the world how we love one another! Let us beam His love with our minds and prayers across the great divides that separate us: our cultures, our languages, our stages of life (old and young) our levels of education and literacy,

---

[6] Give to others, and God will give to you. Indeed, you will receive a full measure, a generous helping, poured into your hands – all that you can hold. The measure you use for others is the one that God will use for you (Luke 6: 38).

[7] The man answered, Love the Lord your God with all your heart, with all your soul, with all your strength, and with all your mind; and Love your neighbor as you love yourself (Luke 10: 27).

[8] Anyone who is not for me is really against me; anyone who does not help me gather is really scattering (Matt. 12: 30).

our degrees of poverty or wealth, our sicknesses or our health, our attitudes to religious beliefs, or our acceptance or rejection of His message. As we beam love consistently, we begin to expand our horizons to see that all people are God's wonderful creations, and He loves them all. He wants to heal and restore them. He asks us to do the same. *He is not looking at their present state so much as what they can become. This is the beginning of how to love as He loves, when we focus on what people can become rather than on how they present themselves at the moment.* When we look for God in them, we will experience the attitude expressed in the hymn that says: 'I see in you the glory of my King and I love you with the love of the Lord' (an attitude that is necessary for unity to happen). Then, we will be required to make a decision to love and not to remain in our isolated ghettos of thinking and speaking messages of negativity that keep us separated. It is urgent that we get this right! Agreed? When we begin to change attitudes and demonstrate this unity, the outside world will be able to see it! It will be easier for the world to hear our message if they see it in our actions.

Will we answer God's call in our time or will we also turn away and continue the present prejudice, isolation, and division? It is our choice. This could be the choice we make for Eternity!

CHAPTER *3*

The Reason for Unity

Imagine that there are two business firms. In one there is harmony between the workers. They know their place and their function, and they are concentrating on doing the best they can to bring forth the product they will eventually sell. They are set on doing their very best for their firm. There is an attitude of peace while they work, content with making their contribution in the very best way they can. There is mutual respect in the air they breathe, which helps them and spurs them on to work harder. They love the product that they will all have had a part in making and are eager to promote the quality and effectiveness of what one day will be sold. There is music in the background as they work, and there is much laughter shared when they take their break for coffee and doughnuts. They are so glad to work and take home with them the knowledge that they did their best that day, so although they are tired, as they put their feet up at home, they are deeply content that they did their bit and did it well. This attitude is like an aura around them as they rest in front of the fire, and it spreads contentment to their children who play on the rug at their feet. There is a happy sense of fulfilment and of time well spent, and when they finally go up to bed, they sleep the sleep of the just and can arise the next day eager to get to work again.

On the other side of the road, there is another factory. It manufactures much the same product, but there is a difference, and it is palpable to those who visit the factory. People often find excuses to stay away from work. Absenteeism is a real problem for the management. People are often sick, and they wonder why they seem to have this problem. They need not look far for the solution. Those who work in this factory are looking at one another critically. Each one is looking for advancement. They are discontented with their little role and are wondering about climbing up the ladder of opportunity to better pay and less arduous work. 'If so-and-so would leave, perhaps I could get his job,' they think. There is competition in the very air they breathe. There is friction between employees, and this is obvious at the breaks when one finds them in small groups usually talking about an absent member. Should that person pass by, there is an unnatural silence until they are out of earshot. Somehow you know if you are not there, they will be talking about you, and it will not be pleasant talk. The employees look at each other critically, sometimes spreading doubtful stories with little truth to back them up. They bring a laugh, though all know the laughter is not from the heart. It rings hollow and leaves a nasty taste behind. This atmosphere is very hard to work in, and they often carry it back home with them and, exhausted, sit by the fire or more often the television. 'Be quiet, children, can't you see how tired I am? I've been working hard for you all day. Now give me a bit of peace. Go away and play,' they snap. The television gives a moment's relief, the favourite sports match and the programme they have been looking forward all day to seeing, for it brings temporary relief from the pressures of daily work. They hate their work, and they bring this resentment home. They are used to criticising so often that the wife gets her share of this negative feeling, and she is criticised too. She retaliates, and soon, there are angry words, which the children pick up and store in their minds. When this family finally goes to bed, they are restless and do not sleep well. When they wake, they are often tired and longing for more time to rest. Another dreary day looms ahead. 'I wonder, is this all there is to life?' they think.

I have painted two pictures of opposite ends of a spectrum of a possible workplace, but these pictures can also represent our churches. *We can easily bring our work atmosphere into our churches.* We can carry what happens to us every day and act the same way when we go to Church. Perhaps we feel the music is too loud, too upbeat, too much, or not enough of the kind we enjoy. We hear the sermon, and we may think, 'Well, I have heard it all before many times. It's nothing new. In fact, if I'm honest, it's boring!' We may share our discontent over the coffee afterwards or even when we talk of our Church to outsiders. *But as in the example of the first workplace, there is another way.* We can desire to contribute, to do our share. We can ask ourselves, 'How can I serve here? What can I offer of my talents? Can I stand at the door and greet people happily? Can I help with the children's ministry? Can I do some ushering at collection time? Can I help at the bookstore? I can sing a bit. Can I join the choir? What can I do to help make it easier for everyone?'

It's all in the attitude we bring with us! Do we spread unity, harmony, and blessing or are we a negative, demanding influence? Do we contribute to the unity of the whole or are we destroying and dividing by judgement, criticism, and complaining? Both these attitudes will be palpable to those around us even if we do not articulate them in words. *People around us feel what is in us!*

I remember going to a home to teach Resurrection Life, to a small group, which is what I do every day. The wife had opened her home to the group and to me, and as I had a long way to drive to get there, she kindly suggested that I could come earlier the following week and dine with her family. I eagerly accepted her generous offer, for she was the only member of her family in the group. We sat down at the table after she had introduced me to her husband and their twenty-year-old son. We talked about this and that, and then there was a pause so I asked a question to get the conversation going again. I said, 'Tell me about your pastor. Can you give me three good adjectives that best describe him, to give me some idea?' I was not expecting what happened! Each of the family kept their eyes on their plate as they silently ate. There was an awkward silence, and finally, the son looked across at me and said, 'We are finding that difficult. Actually, we don't often say anything good about him.' That is a very sad situation, yet it could be multiplied many times. *We, Christians, talk negatively because we think negatively.* This is destructive. Someone once said, 'We are the only organisation who shoots their own wounded!' *What we think is what we become.*

Jesus said, *A family divided against itself falls apart.*[9] Do we contribute or do we detract? Are we a positive force for good or are we undermining each other? What comes out of our mouths is always something we have thought in our minds. Christians are told to think with the mind of Christ.[10] Therefore, for nothing harmful or divisive to come out of our minds, our thoughts need to be taken captive.[11]

---

[9] But Jesus knew what they were thinking, so he said to them, Any country that divides itself into groups which fight each other will not last very long; a family divided against itself falls apart (Luke 11: 17).

[10] As the scripture says, Who knows the mind of the Lord? Who is able to give him advice? We, however, have the mind of Christ (1 Cor. 2: 16).

[11] We pull down every proud obstacle that is raised against the knowledge of God; we take every thought captive and make it obey Christ (2 Cor. 10: 5).

Graphic 5 - Conversion Process in our Minds

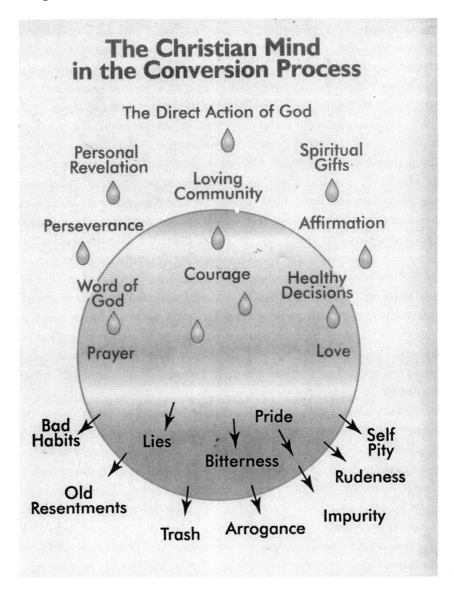

We are responsible for what we let into our minds. We can dismiss a thought and concentrate our attention on something else or we can deliberately choose to harbour a thought and even make a meal of it. It is our choice, a choice that has considerable consequences, for it affects the people around us. A thought occurred to Darwin. He entertained that thought and worked out a whole system built upon it that has influenced thousands of minds and still continues long after his death. Karl Marx sat in a British museum musing on the state of society. He had a thought that he hoped would, if implemented, make a difference in people's lives. It certainly did! We all know the effects of Communism in today's world, yet it started with one thought in the mind of one man.

Our thoughts can have profound consequences. We need to take seriously what thoughts we entertain and rid ourselves of those that hinder the work of God in this world. Jesus is the head of His body, the Church. He is the source of its life.[12] What are we doing to contribute to this Body coming together in love? Let us remember His words, *If a family divides itself into groups which fight each other, that family will fall apart* (Mark 3: 25). Proverbs 29: 11 says, *Stupid people express their anger openly, but sensible people are patient and hold it back.* Jesus tells us to love the Lord with our entire mind, but we can hardly be said to love God as we speak hurtful, divisive things against His Body. Often what we say is based on hearsay, not on researched facts. We can be guilty of harmful gossip about other Christians. Let us be very careful what we spread as *truth* about each other. *If it does not build, let us not say it!*

Satan is very real, and he is totally focused on destroying the Church. He knows that if he can set one person or denomination against another, he is more than halfway to winning. He hates seeing us standing in agreement and will do all in his power to stop that happening. To which voices are we listening? If they divide us from fellow Christians, we can be sure they are not from the Lord.

Jesus commanded us to love one another. He taught us how to live by showing us the way He lived. He was a model of how we should live. He never held resentment even when they told Him He was casting out demons through the power of Beelzebul.[13] (In other words, that He was from satan and not from God.) Imagine how deep that hurt

---

[12] He is the head of his body, the church; he is the source of the body's life (Col. 1: 18a).

[13] When the Pharisees heard this, they replied, He drives out demons only because their ruler Beelzebul gives him power to do so (Matt. 12: 24).

could have gone, but He never allowed people to influence Him negatively. He never let their negativity settle in His heart to cause resentment. He knew they had got things the wrong way round, and His heart went out to them in love and truth; after all, that is why He came to set things right and destroy what the devil had done.[14] He did not retaliate but pleaded with God to forgive them.

So how do we stop talking negatively? It is our choice what we say as it is our choice what we allow to settle in our minds. Satan will put all sorts of suggestions forward and then he will watch to see which of his suggestions we decide to make our own. Then, he will stoke the fire *of that which we have chosen* . . . If we do not resist, satan will keep adding his thoughts, and soon, he will have gotten quite a blaze going within us. In this way, he acquires control of us and can then use us for his own destructive purposes. Is that really what we want? Every choice and every act brings us closer to satan or to Christ. There really is no middle ground. *Anyone who is not for Me is really against Me.*[15]

How did Jesus cope with temptation? In the desert He was alone, taken there immediately by the Holy Spirit, where He was tempted by the devil.[16] Why? His Father had declared publicly who He was at His Baptism. 'You are My own dear Son. I am pleased with you.'[17] Satan challenged this by saying, 'If you are God's Son.'[18] The evil spirit tried to put doubt in Jesus' mind.

---

[14] The Son of God appeared for this very reason, to destroy what the Devil had done (1 John 3: 8b).

[15] Anyone who is not for me is really against me; anyone who does not help me gather is really scattering (Luke 11: 23).

[16] Jesus returned from the Jordan full of the Holy Spirit and was led by the Spirit into the desert, where he was tempted by the Devil for forty days (Luke 4: 1-2a).

[17] and the Holy Spirit came down upon him in bodily form like a dove. And a voice came from heaven, You are my own dear Son. I am pleased with you (Luke 3: 22).

[18] The Devil said to him, If you are God's Son, order this stone to turn into bread (Luke 4: 3).

How did Jesus cope? He quoted Scripture to satan.[19] *He did not try to fight the thought with His own human resources. He used the Word of God: 'The Scripture says . . .'*[20] Why do we know about these temptations at all? We know because Jesus shared them with His disciples. And why did He do that, if not to show us clearly how we, too, are to win over temptations? We must use Scripture. We must not try to fight these thoughts, for they only get bigger if we concentrate on them. Like our Lord, we must set God's truth against satan's lies and move on quickly to think about something else. Every time we do this, we grow stronger in the Lord, stronger to be positive lights and not negative influences. We are changing into who we will become every time we choose Christ or satan, light or darkness, and we will inevitably spread one or the other depending on our choices. So will we stand or will we fall?

As the individual members of the Church stand or fall, so too will the Church! We are one Body, each joined to each. As Scripture says, *Though we are many, we are one Body in union with Christ and we are all joined to each other, different parts of one Body.*[21] When one human cell gets out of sync with the other cells, it easily becomes a tumour. Is that what we want to be in the Body of Christ – cancerous cells? Then, let us ask for God's grace to dismiss every negative thought and replace it with a blessing. As we do this consistently, we will see how quickly the Holy Spirit will transform us on the inside. Soon, other people will be asking what has happened. 'You are different, much easier to get along with!' they will say.

Jesus has said we are like salt for all humankind,[22] like light for the whole world. We are to 'live like people who belong to the

---

[19] But Jesus answered, The scripture says, Human beings cannot live on bread alone, but need every word that God speaks (Matt. 4: 4).

[20] Jesus answered, The scripture says, Worship the Lord your God and serve only him! (Luke 4: 8).

[21] In the same way, though we are many, we are one body in union with Christ, and we are all joined to each other as different parts of one body (Rom. 12: 5).

[22] You are like salt for the whole human race. But if salt loses its saltiness, there is no way to make it salty again. It has become worthless, so it is thrown out and people trample on it (Matt. 5: 13).

light'.[23] Should we be in the second kind of workplace described in this chapter, we are there to make a difference. One candle is small, but it chases away the darkness effectively. Should it join forces with another candle, the light potential will double. At work, why not ask God to put you with another Christian who is lit by the Holy Spirit and start to pray together against the negative darkness in the place? Whole workplaces have changed dramatically in this way. If we do nothing but grumble, nothing will change; in fact, it will get even darker. A believing Christian can make a huge difference – two can defeat 10,000, for God is with them.[24] United we stand, but divided we fall!

What can we, Christians, do to facilitate unity between us? God made us to function together harmoniously so that in some measure we would reflect the unity and purpose of Elohim in whose image we are made. We can do much to bring about this harmony. We can start by clearing away some of the things that continually irritate us about each other, things that have kept us apart for centuries. We may not agree, but at least we can try to understand from where each other is coming. When people are from different language groups, we tend to make considerable allowances as they try to communicate with us. Can we not at least give the same latitude to those who use language which is theologically different from ours? Not that we should change our beliefs, but we can change our attitudes towards others who express their beliefs in ways that seem foreign to us. We use language differently; we mean different things with the words we use.

When I came to America in 1986, I quickly learnt that we, British people, use our English in ways that Americans find quaint and odd. The same words might mean different things depending on from which side of the Atlantic one comes. For instance, the boot of a car is the trunk; the roof is the hood; and the gears

---

[23] You yourselves used to be in the darkness, but since you have become the Lord's people, you are in the light. So you must live like people who belong to the light, for it is the light that brings a rich harvest of every kind of goodness, righteousness, and truth (Eph. 5: 8–9).

[24] Why were a thousand defeated by one, and ten thousand by only two? (Deut. 32: 30a).

are the stick shifts. Tuition in Britain refers to teaching, while in America it means the fees for the teaching. There are many differences, yet we can override them as we get the message behind each and understand its meaning. Can we not give each other the same grace theologically? We do not need to change our opinions, but, at least, we can try to get the message behind how others believe. If we do not jump the hurdle of our language barriers, we will still shun those who do not express things quite like we do. We will not embrace others in unity, but we will be kept aloof in our separateness. Meanwhile, the world looks on and is confused, so it stays away from all of us! If we cling to theology as *the truth*, we can be missing the person of Jesus who is *the Truth. Let us not make the mistake of thinking concepts of truth are the same as Truth itself.*

Let me try to explain this, hopefully, without treading on too many tender toes. Let us just take two examples of how confusion can be maintained between the Protestant and Catholic worlds. This is sensitive ground, so please, Holy Spirit, help me not to add to the present confusion!

1) Our different attitudes towards Mary

Mary was the one woman God chose to become the mother of His Son. No one else has been privileged in this way. It was the unique role she had to play in God's great drama of Redemption. She alone was the mother of Jesus, 'God-made-man'. In Catholic language, they refer to her as *mother of God*. They mean mother of God-made-man, namely Jesus. They are not saying that somehow this elevates her to be mother of the divinity of God. That would be absurd! No! She is a human being designed by God to house Jesus for the nine months that it took for His body to be formed so that He, like us, could be born into this world. She is the mother of Jesus. She is the mother of His humanity, not of His divinity.

But to a Protestant, this phrase, *mother of God*, can conjure up all sorts of understandable resistance. It seems to elevate Mary to a place that is somehow above even God, for in our understanding, mothers beget children! Mothers come first, and then the child follows. To elevate Mary in this way is anathema; it is heresy. It is not the truth of the situation. It is like a red rag to the proverbial

28

bull! If some Catholics seem to elevate Mary in this way, we need to pray for them. Catholic teaching does not support the adoration of Mary. Adoration and worship belongs to God alone. Somehow, in today's world we use these words glibly. We even say, 'I adore you,' when referring to someone we love. The worship of Mary is not at all appropriate language to refer to how Catholics revere her. Worship is only for God. However, we, Christians, are to follow God's own rules concerning parents. Jesus always obeyed God's commandments; therefore, He honours Mary, His earthly mother, and God, His Heavenly Father. *Would He not want us to do the same?* Perhaps the Catholics stress this honouring too much and the Protestants not enough. Perhaps there is a happy medium in between so that we will not use our understanding of Mary to alienate us from each other. God has asked us to be in unity, not division. Perhaps we had better think it out again, asking the Holy Spirit to guide us. Meanwhile, let us be very careful not to alienate each other by the language we use.

Last Sunday, I was in a Church that I greatly respect as being on the cutting edge of listening to the Holy Spirit in today's world. However, the pastor who was preaching said that Catholics *worship* Mary, and Protestants do not respect her sufficiently. He was referring to the opposite poles of this spectrum, and he was suggesting a middle ground of possibility. *Great,* I thought, but the use of the word *worship* jarred me. To both a Catholic and a Protestant, worship is for God alone. Catholics do not *worship* Mary; they honour and respect her in the role that God gave to her and which she so beautifully fulfilled. Throughout the New Testament, we see that Mary was there in the background. She was at His death and at His birth. She was in the upper room when God poured out His Spirit at Pentecost. Mary played a unique role in this great saga. It was through her that Jesus came, so let us love and honour her but not give her worship or adoration, which is reserved for God alone. Words can unite, or they can divide. Let us be careful in our use of them!

2) The different ways we pray

The second point that I would like to try to bring clarity to is in some ways tied to the above. 'Protestants pray straight to

Jesus, so why do Catholics pray to Mary and the saints?' I have heard this question asked many times. To try to answer this, may I ask some questions? What is our understanding of family? Do those who have gone on before us still belong to our family? Is our family limited to just those who are alive right now?

The Catholic understanding of God's family includes those who, in this life, have fulfilled their destinies through His grace at work in their lives and those whom God has taken straight to heaven. Enoch, Elijah, and the good thief are examples in Scripture. Catholics believe that Jesus took Mary straight to heaven in the same way. Surely, it would have been in keeping with His desire to honour His mother for Jesus to do so. There is no reference to this in Scripture, but John declares if everything that Jesus did was written down, no book could contain it. So it is possible that Jesus does raise some to heaven directly. Maybe the Father took Mary to heaven; we do not know, but Catholics believe she is now in heaven with Jesus. So it is not that Catholics pray to the dead. No, those in heaven are living, perhaps more fully than we are down here. They are living in the glory of heaven, close to the very throne of God. When you want someone to pray for you, whom do you choose? Surely, you choose someone you trust and who you think is close to God. Catholics do the same, but they see God's family as including those in heaven, as well as those on earth! Can we not allow each other to see differently rather than use these differences as a reason or even a weapon to keep us apart? Catholics, just like Protestants, usually pray directly to Jesus or to God, the Heavenly Father, or to the Holy Spirit. In their deep spiritual lives, their focus is on God, the provider of all good gifts. Personal petition, or asking prayer, is a small part of any Christian's prayer life. Repentance, thanksgiving, praise, adoration, worship, and intercession for God's Kingdom to come on earth make up the main focus in any Christian's dialogue with God, no matter in which denomination they have settled. Surely, we can come together to pray in these ways in union rather than use liturgical prayers with which not all of us can feel comfortable. Let us leave what could divide us for our personal prayer time and use prayers that unite us when we pray corporately. God listens to our hearts as we pray, not to our forms of prayer. Can we not at least try to do the same?

I offer these thoughts, not to justify our differences, but to try to pour oil on what has been used to keep the Body of Christ apart. Satan wants us to argue and be resentful of each other. He will do much to keep us from uniting. Why does he do that? Because if we are exhibiting love for each other and are united in praying against the evils that are around us, we will become the most lethal weapon against which satan and his evil hoard cannot stand. He will do a great deal to stop us uniting in this way. Let us not let him succeed in our generation. *United we stand and he falls! Alleluia!*

Division is not confined to denomination or theology. It is misunderstanding that often alienates us from each other. This misunderstanding may enter into our relationships in general and to marriage in particular. Divorce is currently at an all-time high among Christians as well as non-Christians. It is the opposite of unity. In our teaching at RLM, we put on a skit to illustrate this. Two men meet after some time apart. This is their conversation:

Bill: Hello, Henry, long time no see, eh! How are things with you?

Henry: Good, Bill. My! But it is quite some time since we met. It is good to see you again.

Bill: Henry, I heard you got married. Is that so?

Henry: Yes, we have been married just three months now, and it's good. There's nothing like marriage to meet a guy's needs. I think it's going well because I sat the little wife down that very night and explained to her just what to expect. Get it right from the start. Then they know where they are. That's what I say. Give it to them straight!

Bill: What did you tell her, Henry?

Henry: I told her what I expected of her now that she was my wife. I said, 'Now, my dear, I just want to get things straight from the start. I expect my shirts ironed and ready, the house cleaned and tidy when I come home, good food on the table, just how I like it, and, of course, my needs taken care of when we go to bed. That goes without saying. Now do these things and you will have a happy man on your hands. Understand?'

Bill: What did she say, Henry?

Henry: Well, she did not say anything. She just looked at me a bit dumbfounded. I suppose I took her by surprise, but that's me, straight to the point, no beating around the bush.

Bill: Henry, can I ask you a question?

Henry: Of course, you can. Ask away!

Bill: Are you a Christian, Henry?

Henry: Christian, oh, yes. I go to Church on Sunday and all that sort of thing. In fact, we go together. But what has that got to do with it?

Bill: Do you believe that we should be doing what Jesus told us to do? I mean He gave us some guidelines about how we should treat our wives and how to make our marriages work. He said that marriage was the union of two equal human beings. Our wives would be subject to us as we were subject to Him. That love between husband and wife would be demonstrated by their unity. Men were to show their wives love in the same way as He gave Himself for His Church. He said, if we loved our wives in His way, they would respond freely in their love to us. There is a lot to all this, and we all need to understand it better, don't we? There is a group of us men who meet every week and share together how we can put what Jesus said into practice better.

Henry: Well, Bill, I was doing what I saw my father do. I mean, at home, he laid down the law pretty strong and we all jumped to attention. That was how it was at home, so I thought that is the way it should be. Actually, I didn't know Jesus had something to say about all this. I suppose it would be good to know about that. When do these groups of yours meet?

Bill: We have an early breakfast together on Tuesday morning at 6.30 a.m. We have found it very useful because we are all learning about how our marriages can work better. If you would like to come, we would love to have you join us. Think about it. Here's the address should you decide to come.

Henry: You know, Bill, I might. I am glad we met today. I'll think about all this. Perhaps you'll see me next Tuesday. Bye for now.

It is always interesting to notice the reactions of the audience when we do this little skit. We realise that people understand where we are coming from all too well! God made marriage to illustrate His love and unity.

Graphic 6 – Marriage

The wonder of unity

God is in perfect unity. Elohim (Father, Son, and Holy Spirit) are a unity of love. *We are made in God's image, and we are called to reflect Their unity, even while here on earth.* Jesus said that when we come to Church to worship Him together, if we are not in unity with someone, we should follow Christ's teaching, *so if you are about to offer your gift to God at the altar and there you remember that your brother has something against you, leave your gift there in front of the altar, go at once and make peace with your brother, and then come back and offer your gift to God* (Matt. 5: 23–24). Our worship must demonstrate our peace with each other. Unity is extremely important to God. We cannot love without it.

I think it is the same in marriage, which is given to us to express the unity of husband and wife. I think the same principle applies. If we are not one in mind and heart in our marriage, we should not consummate our union sexually until we have sorted out the problem between us. *Sex was meant to be the icing on the cake of unity. But one does not have icing if there is no cake!* Sex was never intended to be the right of one partner over the other, a nightly ritual that would resolve all difficulties. If we use it in that way, it ceases to have the wondrous lustre of a joy-filled gift, one to the other. It becomes a ritual, just like our worship can also become routine.

I think both these wonderful gifts of God are meant to express the unity of love. Worship and sex are awesome when we are in unity, one with the other. They are meant to express this unity. Worship is our gift to God for the wonder of who He is and the marvel of the relationship He is offering us. Sex is the marital equivalent, for it is the expression of our gift to each other of all that we are. When we are one in mind and heart, then it truly expresses this, and it binds us together in ever-closer ways. Treated like this, sex will not lose its novelty, and it will never become just something we do every night or when the mood suits us. We can demean sex if it does not genuinely reflect our unity. We need to get the unity right. Then the sex will properly reflect it for both parties. *Love is always reflected through unity. They are inseparable.*

Whether it is our workplace, Church, marriage, or family, Christians are there to demonstrate unity. *That is why it is so important for us to value this unity or we will not reflect it.*

CHAPTER 4

Unity as a Weapon

In November 2004, Americans went to the polls and cast their votes for who they wanted to lead this country for the next four years. Both candidates had spent much time and many resources to gain these votes. When we are voting together in one direction, we will see victory. America decided in which direction it would be going for the next four years. Prior to the election, there was much talk and prayer to get all the voters out to vote. Why? *Because each vote counts.* President Bush won the 2000 election by the very small margin of just 500 votes. What if those 500 people had decided to stay at home? Every vote counts, especially when the candidates are seen as equally matched.

It is the same spiritually. We all have twenty-four hours every day, and we have all been chosen by God, our designer, to make a contribution during our lifetime on earth. He wants to know who we are voting for – ourselves or His Son. Christ has chosen us, but will we consistently choose Him, day in and day out? Is it His priorities that we are most concerned about or our own? Jesus told us to *be concerned above everything else with the Kingdom of God and with what He requires of you, and He will provide you with all these other things.*[25] Selfishness is a deeply ingrained force within us. We are born into this world kicking and screaming, 'Take care of me.' Babies are totally self-centred. In fact, this is necessary for their survival. We learn that we need to defend ourselves in childhood, and this can be carried over into adulthood. We are ruled by self-interest, the Me, Myself, and I trilogy! That is the natural state of humankind – we are self-centred.

But Christ has called us to a higher way – we must be born again.[26] We must be born in the Spirit and develop into the spiritual beings God first designed us to be. The only way out of our ingrained natural self-preoccupation is to grow in our preoccupation with God and His purposes. We cannot do this until the Holy Spirit has ignited us spiritually, and we are born again in the Spirit. Let us ask and it will be given to us.[27] Then, we need to put our natural selves on hold while we allow God to lead us into the most exciting adventure possible, that of drawing close to Him and learning the ways of His Spirit. This journey of adventure is fuelled by faith, whereas the natural person is controlled by reason. Living by faith is a higher way to live, but we are to choose this way together. We cannot do it alone.

Unity involves oneness with God and oneness with each other.[28] This is not possible in the natural. God is spirit, so it is

---

[25] Instead, be concerned above everything else with the Kingdom of God and with what he requires of you, and he will provide you with all these other things (Matt. 6: 33).

[26] Jesus answered, 'I am telling you the truth: no one can see the Kingdom of God without being born again.' 'How can a grown man be born again?' Nicodemus asked. 'He certainly cannot enter his mother's womb and be born a second time!' I am telling you the truth, replied Jesus, that no one can enter the Kingdom of God without being born of water and the Spirit. A person is born physically of human parents, but is born spiritually of the Spirit. Do not be surprised because I tell you that you must all be born again (John 3: 3–7).

[27] If you believe, you will receive whatever you ask for in prayer (Matt. 21: 22).

[28] I pray that they may all be one. Father! May they be in us, just as you are in me and I am in you. May they be one, so that the world will believe that you sent me (John 17: 21).

only with our spirits that unity with Him can occur. It is not something we can effect just by willing it to happen, although that might be a good way to start! We are not able to do so because it is spiritual, and we function naturally. However, when we are willing, the Holy Spirit teaches us this new way to live. Every step of this journey is a step of faith. Peter is, as usual, a good example for us.

Imagine that you are one of the disciples in the boat going across the Sea of Galilee. Jesus is left behind on the other shore, but He has told you to go to the other side. It is dark and cold, and you are taking turns controlling the boat and empowering it to make headway across the waters. Suddenly, one of you sees someone approaching the boat, seemingly walking on the water. Surely, no one can do this. You strain your eyes to get a better vision. Yes, the person is coming closer, and it is someone walking on the water! Unbelievable!

Peter takes the lead. He knows no one can do this naturally. He wonders if this could be his Lord Jesus. *Lord! If it is You, bid me come to You across the water.* They all hear clearly Christ's answer, *It is. Come.* Impetuous Peter starts to clamber out of the boat. His feet touch the cold night waters, and *yes*, he starts to walk, looking only at Jesus.

Then his natural mind and experience set in. This can't be happening, he thinks. No one can walk on water. At once Peter's focus shifts from Jesus to himself and his own experience of life, and at once he starts to sink. In desperation, he cries out to Jesus to save him, and Jesus does saying, *What little faith you have! Why did you doubt?*[29]

The way of the Spirit is contrary to our natural experience. Every time circumstances surround us, and they look to our natural eyes as impossible, we are living Peter's experience. Like him, we have a choice to make. Do we choose to see it God's way or do we choose to rely on our natural experience?

---

[29] At once Jesus reached out and grabbed hold of him and said, What little faith you have! Why did you doubt? (Matt. 14: 31)

Graphic 7 - God's and Our Ways of Seeing

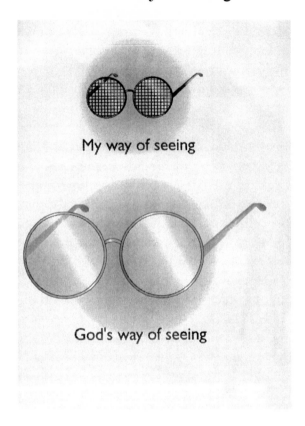

Do we count on God, or do we retreat into our own experiences of what is possible? Walking in faith and not sight is the only way to grow in the spirit, for it is contrary to our natural flesh. We must choose to put the natural on hold while we venture out into this faith version of living. Yes, it is scary. Yes, it will take us to the end of our selfishness, but it is the only way to live in God's way. The more impossible things seem, the more we seek to trust God, and He always stretches out His hand to save us, as He did for Peter. *If you have a problem, do not fight it. Look for God in it, for He is there. Find Him, put Him in charge, and the problem will melt.*

Just as each believer must learn personally to trust God in their own lives, so too must we, corporately, as the Church. There is a spiritual war going on around us. The forces of evil are escalating, showing themselves clearly to be what they are. There is a steadily increasing suicide rate, which is far more prevalent than when I was a child. There is destruction of innocent lives at a scale that would have been seen to be impossible only a few years ago. Children are being deceived into truly believing it is glorious to blow themselves up and take as many people with them as possible. Terrorism is in all countries, trying to make people afraid, insecure, and unstable. The stability of the God-given norm for marriage is being threatened. The way God designed one to be is now being dismissed, and people are being taught one can choose whether one is male or female. Doctors are being sued when they refuse to impregnate lesbian women. Judges can be usurping the Constitution and deciding on their own what is right or wrong. Are we the judges of what is right and wrong or are there God-given guidelines which He has communicated to us? Evil is escalating around us and will engulf us if we try to fight it on our own with natural weapons. *The Church is called on to make a stand together,* to put our self-centred projects on hold while we come together in unity with the Lord and with each other. We are at war, but the battle can only be won by us using spiritual weapons *together.*

Neither is the Church a conglomerate of different denominations, nor is it one particular denomination. It is all Christians across denominational barriers that worship God – Father, Son, and Holy Spirit – and recognise Jesus as God's solution to all the evil in the world, knowing that, through His death, He has enabled us to come into God's supernatural life. It is this Church worldwide on which Jesus has poured out His Spirit, empowering it to go forth in His name, in obedience and in unity, and see evil defeated. When we do this, we are truly the light of the world and the salt of the earth. But it is our choice whether we use His power and authority in obedience to Him and rejoice in seeing His Kingdom spread and evil retreat. *Our weapons are unity of focus and obedience in prayer.* When we are thus united, God has promised to protect us. *But no weapon will be able to hurt you.*[30] We are called for such a time as this! Will we stand for Christ, actively joining other

---

[30] But no weapon will be able to hurt you; you will have an answer for all who accuse you. I will defend my servants and give them victory. The Lord has spoken (Isa. 54: 17).

Christians who may not worship as we do, agree with our theology completely or act like us? *We pray with Jesus, standing over evil.*

Graphic 8 - Praying with Christ

When I was a little girl, I lived in Wales. Like other children, I picked up what was around me. In those days, bigotry was rampant. I was a Protestant, and we were in open hostility with the Catholic children, even to the extent of attacking each other with rulers. In my ignorance, I led one such combat until the police were called in and stopped it. Did we know what we were doing or why we felt this animosity? No! We picked it up from the adults around us. I was eleven years old when this problem exploded in my otherwise dignified and caring family. I did not understand why Christians were fighting each other. It made no sense at all to me. My mother decided to become a Catholic, to which the family reacted in anger. When we, children, were sent to bed, all hell broke loose in our living room. My brother and I sat on the top stair listening intently. My grandfather, whom I had never seen angry before, was so enraged that he slammed the front door saying he would never darken it again. He left. Normally gentle aunts came by and actually slapped my mother to bring her to her senses. I had never seen adults behave in this way before. 'Why, God, why are they doing this?' I cried silently. I knew God as my Father, and I had a very personal way of talking with Him whom I trusted completely. I ran into His arms for protection and comprehension. But I distrusted the kind of Christianity that would manifest in this way. *They must have got it wrong,* I concluded.

My dear grandmother, a strong but gentle soul, called me one day, sometime after this episode. This is what she had to say, 'Molly, you are our last hope. I want you to do something that may stop your mother from making the biggest mistake in her life. Molly, she is in great danger. It is as though she is caught in a spiderweb like a little unsuspecting fly. She is caught there, and the spider is descending on her, ready to make a meal of her. The spider is the Catholic Church, and it will take all our money and destroy our family. Please, Molly, you are our last hope. I want you to go to your mother and plead on your knees with her, even to tears, that she does not do this dreadful thing of becoming a Catholic.'

I went to my mother and did my best. After all, she was in danger! I had no idea what it was all about. But my mother, bless her, realised what was happening. She was gentle with me as she said that what she was doing was her own affair – she would tell me later it was the best thing she had ever done – and that I was not to become a Catholic just because she had. I was free to worship anywhere I chose as long as I went to Church somewhere on Sunday. That set me looking for the right expression of Church, and I explored everything that came my way. I learnt a lot. Above all, I was looking for people who lived God's Great

41

Commandment – to love God and each other. I was eleven years old. This search became my focus.

I learnt that there are many expressions of Christianity, but none have it all. We need each other, for only together can we each bring our particular strength to the whole, while rejoicing in the strengths of others that compensate for our weaknesses. Together, it works. So what can we learn from each other?

I learnt that the *Catholics* have a deep understanding of silent worship, of awe in the presence of Father God. They understand the meaning of suffering when it is united to the sufferings of Christ. They have a great loyalty to the Catholic Church. They understand obedience to authority and collective humble unity. They teach that whatever you do to the least of His little ones, you do to Jesus. That was evidenced clearly in Mother Teresa's life. A Protestant recently asked me if I thought Mother Teresa was a Christian!

The *Evangelicals* understand outreach to the lost, and they stress bringing people to Christ individually through a decision. They are committed to the Lord Jesus in a complete and purposeful way to bring about His Kingdom here on earth. A personal relationship with Jesus, and evangelising others to receive it, is vital to them. Many evangelicals do not think Catholics can be Christian, and they believe that one must leave the Catholic Church and join theirs! When I went to an evangelistic training centre for a year, they tried hard to convert me, not realising that I had been introduced to Jesus personally over forty years previously, when I became a Catholic!

The *Pentecostals* are strongly committed to the Holy Spirit and teach powerfully the evidencing in life of the gifts and then the fruits of the Spirit. They teach that, as we are in a spiritual battle, only spiritual weapons are truly effective. This aspect of Church is growing faster than any other at present.

The *Presbyterians* emphasise the sovereignty of God and the wonder of His Kingdom. They revere scholarship and doctrinal purity, and they stress the relevance of preaching the Word of God as applied to everyday life.

The *Methodists* are strong on providing a caring community for newly evangelised people to join. They love hymn singing and fellowship.

The *Quakers* practise silent, Spirit-led prayer, and equal leadership through men and women. They stress holy living, which is much needed in today's world.

The *Mennonites* teach that it is not only receiving Christ as Lord and Saviour but also remaining true to Him to death that matters. He calls us to become His disciples, and this is a lifelong commitment.

The *Baptists* stress the necessity of following the Lord's instructions and being baptised. It is not just a question of going under the physical water, but Baptism is a symbol of the wonder of being spiritually regenerated. One leaves behind the old life and arises a new creation in Christ.

The *Lutherans* stress that it is our reception of God's gift of His grace, not our works that enables us to enter into spiritual life. Recognition of God's wonderful gift of life is the mainspring of their worship and the bedrock of their faith. Doing everything in the name of Jesus is seen as very important.

The *Anglicans* try not to exclude anyone. Tolerance is very important to them. All are acceptable to God because all are sinners. All need redemption into Christ alike. The Holy Spirit will sort out our sin as He enlightens each of us, and we repent. It is, therefore, not for us to judge and exclude those God has called to join us.

Each Church has its own forte, its own gift to bring to the complete expression of Christ's Church on earth. God is working on us all to bring about His unity. *We need each other, for we are all cells of His body, totally reliant on Jesus, our head, to bring us into the miracle of unity. Let us see the good in each other that we may learn from each other's strengths and step aside from the weaknesses we all exhibit.*

I see two mighty hands, the hands of Christ's Body. Each hand is functioning on its own at present – Catholics in their way and Protestants in theirs. Rarely do these hands agree to work together. Why not? We all know we can do much more using both hands. The hands are similar, yet different. Why cannot these two great hands cooperate to bring in the harvest and extend the Kingdom of God? *These hands can fold together in prayer or be clenched separately as fists.* Understanding each other is necessary for there to be even the possibility of accepting that we can pray in unity.

The Baptist pastor I referred to in Chapter 2, who evangelised with the Catholic friar in Mexico City, told how he had had a prejudice against how Catholics prayed the rosary until he understood what they were doing. It is a prayer form that unified peasant people in prayer before any could read and was a strong tool for evangelism in the Dark Ages. He explained how he had seen it as praying to Mary and not to Jesus and as such had rejected it as a prayer tool. Then it was explained to him what was actually going on in this prayer, and he was filled with wonder at the variety of prayer God has given His Church throughout the centuries. *He went on to explain to the conference the new understanding and respect he had for those who prayed in this way. The gist of what he said is as follows:*

We are easily distracted when we try to pray, and the beads help to keep our focus physically. Each bead is a said prayer, which is the salutation of the angel to Mary at the Incarnation: Hail Mary full of grace. *But that is not the heart of the prayer.* There are *twenty short meditations* as one mentally recites the Hail Mary, thus keeping focused while the heart and spirit can wonder at each of these mysteries in turn. The *five joyful mysteries* of the early childhood of the Lord are the Incarnation (conception) of Jesus, the Visitation to Elizabeth, the Birth of Jesus, the Circumcision of Jesus, and the Finding of Jesus in the temple (His Bar Mitzvah). The five *luminous mysteries* are the Baptism of Jesus in the Jordan, Jesus converts water into wine at Cana, Jesus proclaims the coming of the Kingdom of God with his call to conversion, the Transfiguration of Jesus, and Jesus institutes the Eucharist. The *five sorrowful mysteries* of Jesus are the Agony in Gethsemane, the Scourging at the pillar, the Crowning with thorns, the Carrying of the cross, and the Crucifixion. The *five glorious mysteries* are the Resurrection of Jesus, His Ascension, Pentecost, the Assumption (the meeting again in heaven of Mary and Jesus), and finally, the Glorious Climax of all the saints in heaven at the end of this huge drama of God. *'While I cannot as yet pray like this,' the Baptist pastor said, 'I can at last respect those who can.'*

If we understand each other better, we will not reject each other and continue the divisions of prejudice. Prejudice says, 'Unless you look like me, I will reject you.' God answers heartfelt, honest, humble prayer from all of us. It might look different to us, but how He sees our prayer is what matters! Why not ask Him? Let us learn how He loves all His children equally and join together in His love.

I have been greatly encouraged recently by three happenings that evidence the unity we can show to the world. First, whenever there is a natural disaster, a tsunami or the appalling typhoon that swept across the Philippines demolishing homes and leaving innumerable people without the basics of life, shelter, food, water, sanitation, and medical and emotional help . . ., there is a worldwide response. People who were absorbed in their own problems change the direction of their priorities and putting their own need to one side, dig deep into their resources to help others in a far worse plight. The response has been real, heartfelt, and generous. It makes one glad to belong to the human race and lifts us all from grumbling to gratitude.

Second, in 2006 I saw evidence of a wonderful unity. People from all walks of life joined together and gave freely of their time and energy to bring about the Billy Graham meeting in the Rose Bowl, in Los Angeles County. People cheerfully did their bit to make the whole a success. And it was! Over 4,000 people gave their lives to follow Jesus, and there were many thousands who recommitted their lives to Him. It was the only time Billy Graham asked to present a meeting as he was eighty-five years old and he had started his ministry in Los Angeles in 1949. Billy Graham evidences a life totally given to bringing everyone to the wonder of God's love as seen in the cross of Christ. The stadium was filled to capacity on the Saturday meeting, with 90,000 people praising God together in the cold night air. *There was unity evidenced among Christians, and there, too, was its fruit, with thousands accepting Jesus as their Way forward. Now it is up to the Church to help these people grow.*

Billy Graham is still alive today at 96 years of age. He was spiritual adviser to seven American presidents, involved in the civil rights movement and even bailed Martin Luther King Jr. out of jail in the 1960s when King was arrested in demonstrations. He has been a beacon light flashing hope in a pretty dark world. I thank God for people like him, for his courage, perseverance, and passion for God that have kept him strong into his nineties.

The third consolation to the ache in my heart to see unity functioning among us is Christmas. Every year the whole of the Christian world thinks about *goodwill to all people* when they celebrate Christmas. Often, I have heard people say, 'If only we could think this goodwill all the year round and not just at Christmas!' Yet every year it seems, when the season fades, so too does our goodwill! The encouraging part is that it always re-emerges as the festive season approaches again.

Christmas has much to teach us, and perhaps each year these realisations deepen in our hearts to bring us nearer to what God desires, namely *Peace on earth and goodwill to all men.* God loves all people especially those caught in darkness. We were all caught up in our own selfishness, for without His gift of new life, we could not change. He came to give us the chance of living beyond our natural restrictive confines. He came to lift us up to understand what real love is all about and to join Him in loving in this way. He came to give us the gift that would enable this change to take place. He came in a way that would draw us to Him without fear. He came as a tiny dependent baby. He came as Jesus. He trusted Himself into the hands of Mary and Joseph and grew in wisdom and grace just like any little baby does. *What an incredible wonder this is! His destiny was to reconcile all of us to God.*

As the hymns we all sing at Christmas annually remind us,

> 'Hark the herald angels sing,
> Glory to the new-born King.
> Peace on earth and mercy mild,
> *God and sinners reconciled.*
> Joyful all you nations rise,
> Join the triumph of the skies.
> With the angelic host proclaim,
> Christ is born in Bethlehem.'

As we sing these verses together, *our hearts can lighten towards Him or tighten against Him.* As we believe in the wonder of God's gift, so too are we drawn into His way of loving, and our hearts expand. Or like the Dickens's character, Scrooge, in his classic story, *A Christmas Carol,* we withdraw into the darkness of our own little hearts saying, 'Humbug! Poppycock!' We scoff at the merriment and generosity around us. Our hearts harden and shrivel in unbelief. It is our choice! *But there is a third possibility.* We can trivialise the whole wonder and miss it. It can mean to us just a time of rushing about, spending money on what we think others might want. We can get caught up in the partying and drinking and end up frustrated, even resenting the whole idea of Christmas. We can miss God's gift year after year. There can still be *no room for Him to be born in our inn!* Just as it was 2,000 years ago, so, too, can it be today for each one of us. Jesus invites us to celebrate life with Him. He is the most generous, fun-loving expression of God's goodness there is. He wants families to come together, for all differences to be reconciled, for forgiveness to triumph over fractions and for peace, love, and joy to flourish worldwide. He came to make this possible, and He wants His Church to show the world how His family should function. That is why unity between us is imperative. If the world sees us exhibiting disunity, if it sees us divided, selfishly guarding our own denominational territory, it will stay away. If it sees us exhibiting generosity and goodwill to all people groups, showing open-hearted love, sharing what we have with those in need, it will be drawn to the authentic expression of what the Babe of Bethlehem came to show us. I believe God is calling us at this time in history to be this authentic expression.

He is about to draw all people to Him. We could well be at the time of the Great Harvest when His Spirit will sweep the earth looking for those who will receive Him. He calls everyone. There is no one too far gone or too hopeless. He is love itself, and nothing can be too difficult for Him to rectify. He is calling, and He wants us, His Church, to be the arms that welcome and the hearts that flow out to receive people different from ourselves but equally loved by Him. For this purpose we were created. For this time we were sent into the world. We are His ambassadors. Let the world see at last in us His love for one another. Then it can begin to believe that we may be able to love them too. As Jesus came to reconcile all sinners to God, could our destiny be that we are a visible sign of that reconciliation? If the world does not see that in us, we are not living our true destiny. Could we pray about this now together?

> 'Father God, unite us in Your love so that we are a demonstration of Your love to the world. Lord, show us how to receive others as You receive us so that we will receive all those You are calling from the darkness of the world to Your glorious life. Draw them to You through us, Lord. Adapt us so that we may treat them as You want them treated. Enable us to give up anything that blocks Your perfect will to be done now on earth as it is already done in heaven. Blow away, mighty Spirit of God, any hindrances we cherish, any traditions that we idolise, that could block Your perfect transformation of Your Church for Your perfect will to be accomplished now in our time. This we ask in Jesus' name.'

If we look at the things that keep us apart, we are continuing the division of centuries, but if we recognise the different strengths and learn humbly from each other, we can come into mutual respect, though perhaps not theological agreement. We can listen and understand how *God is wanting us to join together to fight the common foe, evil in the world.* If we choose to stay rigidly in our fortified denominations, we can miss what God wants to be done in our lifetime, for God is breaking down the barriers between us and stretching out our hands to come together to pray against the enemy forces. He is using stadiums to bring us all together to pray together. Will we cooperate and open our hearts to Him and to His people? The escalation of evil in our day is forcing us to come together to make a stand for Christ in today's world. As always, God is turning the evil around for His own divine purposes. Alleluia!

One such evil that can help us to fight as a united, resolute army is the hideous slaughter of the unborn. Here are some statistics to give us an idea of the extent of the problem: From 1973 through 2011, nearly 53 million legal abortions occurred in the US. Half of pregnancies among American women are unintended; about 4 in 10 of these are terminated by abortion. 21% of all U.S. pregnancies (excluding miscarriages) end in abortion. The US abortion rate is similar to those of Australia, New Zealand, and Sweden but higher than those of other Western European countries. (source: www.abort73.com) For women resident in England and Wales in 2013 185,331 abortions took place plus another 5,469 for women who were not residents. These numbers were the lowest total in any year since 1969. (source: www.gov.uk). Each of these babies was created by God. Each was made in His image, and yet we dare to kill them mercilessly. When there is a slaughter of adults, there is a huge shout of protest. Why is there a silence when the weakest of all, the unborn child, is slaughtered? *It is time that the whole Church arises as one Body and demands justice for the unborn child, one voice echoing the heart of God their creator, one voice, His Body, demanding to be heard.* This kind of unity will soon make a difference as we cry, 'Enough is enough! Stop the killing!'

However, while we can agree to stand against the evil of abortion globally, we also need to remember with compassion the trauma of mind of those who seek this solution is great. Each woman facing this decision goes through much soul-searching and we Christians can offer them ministry to alleviate their pain, for God will take all aborted children to Himself. They are not lost, nor does God want us to be burdened by guilt and shame. Giving the problem to Him can give us His resolution of our suffering. None of us are here to judge, are we?

United, we are an end-time army that nothing can withstand. When we pray together and when we use God's spiritual weapons together focused on the evil we are destroying, then we will see results. *United, persistent, focused prayer is essential.* This kind of prayer requires unity of purpose and resolute determination to see victory happen.

Graphic 9 - Laser Beam Prayer

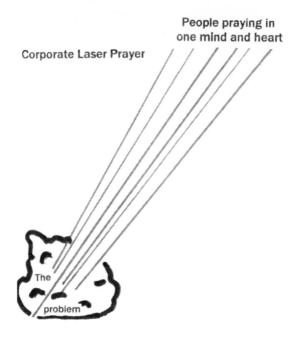

When we all pray like this, there will be results. Then the world will see a Church they may want to join! The world will be forced to choose between the escalating evil and the fear it brings or the Gospel message that brings hope and purpose as evidenced by the unity of Christians. There will be much persecution, even as there was in the first three centuries of the Church's life. But God preserved His Church then and He will now, for when we seek Him in the secret place, He will cover us with His mighty wings.[31]

God has promised that *I will build my Church, and not even death will ever be able to overcome it,*[32] and we count on the total assurance we have in His promises. They cannot fail, for He is God!

———————

———————

[31] Whoever goes to the Lord for safety, whoever remains under the protection of the Almighty, can say to him, You are my defender and protector. You are my God; in you I trust. He will keep you safe from all hidden dangers and from all deadly diseases. He will cover you with his wings; you will be safe in his care; his faithfulness will protect and defend you. You need not fear any dangers at night or sudden attacks during the day or the plagues that strike in the dark or the evils that kill in daylight. A thousand may fall dead beside you, ten thousand all around you, but you will not be harmed. You will look and see how the wicked are punished. You have made the Lord your defender, the Most High your protector, and so no disaster will strike you, no violence will come near your home. God will put his angels in charge of you to protect you wherever you go. They will hold you up with their hands to keep you from hurting your feet on the stones. You will trample down lions and snakes, fierce lions and poisonous snakes. God says, I will save those who love me and will protect those who acknowledge me as Lord. When they call to me, I will answer them; when they are in trouble, I will be with them. I will rescue them and honor them. I will reward them with long life; I will save them (Ps. 91: 1–16).

[32] And so I tell you, Peter: you are a rock, and on this rock foundation I will build my church, and not even death will be ever be able to overcome it (Matt. 16: 18).

CHAPTER 5

Unity as a Healing Balm

God Wants All People Healed and Restored to Their Proper Dignity

God is indeed in charge of His Church and His world. He has given us all a safe road on which to travel. It does wind through dark valleys and is often steep to climb, but it is totally safe. That road is Jesus, who declared, *I am the way, the truth, and the life.*[33]

As Isaiah says:

> *The desert will rejoice, and flowers will bloom in the wastelands. The desert will sing and shout for joy; it will be as beautiful as the Lebanon Mountains and as fertile as the fields of Carmel and Sharon. Everyone will see the Lord's splendor, see his greatness and power. Give strength to hands that are tired and to knees that tremble with weakness. Tell everyone who is discouraged, Be strong and don't be afraid! God is coming to your rescue, coming to punish your enemies. The blind will be able to see, and the deaf will hear. The lame will leap and dance, and those who cannot speak will shout for joy. Streams of water will flow through the desert; the burning sand will become a lake,*

---

[33] Jesus answered him, 'I am the way, the truth, and the life; no one goes to the Father except by me.' (John 14: 6)

*and dry land will be filled with springs. Where jackals used to
live, marsh grass and reeds will grow. There will be a highway
there, called The Road of Holiness. No sinner will ever travel
that road; no fools will mislead those who follow it. No lions will
be there; no fierce animals will pass that way. Those whom the
Lord has rescued will travel home by that road. They will reach
Jerusalem with gladness, singing and shouting for joy. They
will be happy forever, forever free from sorrow and grief (Isa.
35: 1–10).*

The road to holiness (wholeness) is Christ, and He is pouring
out His Holy Spirit on anyone who has ears to hear and a heart
to listen. In Him is our unity. *Unity and love go hand in hand. They
cannot be separated.* Surely, we are in agreement with Paul as he
prays for his friends and for us who will come after:

*The Spirit is the guarantee that we shall receive what God has
promised his people, and this assures us that God will give
complete freedom to those who are his. Let us praise his glory!
For this reason, ever since I heard of your faith in the Lord
Jesus and your love for all of God's people, I have not stopped
giving thanks to God for you. I remember you in my prayers
and ask the God of our Lord Jesus Christ, the glorious Father,
to give you the Spirit, who will make you wise and reveal God
to you, so that you will know him. I ask that your minds may
be opened to see his light, so that you will know what is the hope
to which he has called you, how rich are the wonderful blessings
he promises his people, and how very great is his power at work
in us who believe. This power working in us is the same as the
mighty strength which he used when he raised Christ from death
and seated him at his right side in the heavenly world. Christ
rules there above all heavenly rulers, authorities, powers, and
lords; he has a title superior to all titles of authority in this
world and in the next. God put all things under Christ's feet and
gave him to the Church as supreme Lord over all things (Eph.
1: 14–22).*

*The Church and Jesus are to work together to see the Father's great plan
executed on this earth.* What a privilege! Together, we are the healing
for the nations. The blind will see, the deaf will hear, just as it
happened when Jesus Himself healed. He will heal through us. It is

happening today, both inside and outside the Church, as we go out to the workplace or the shopping malls in Jesus' name and under His obedience. He will heal as we tend to those within our lives who have been deeply scarred by the wounds they have received. God longs to heal and build us up, and He uses human, Spirit-led people to do this, for the deepest wounds can only be healed by His Spirit. That is why some therapists bring their clients to us in Resurrected Life Ministries. They recognise that the deep problems are spiritual.

In the seventies, the Holy Spirit poured out His truth and power through the Charismatic Renewal in Britain. God removed the blinders from our eyes, and we saw Christianity in a different light. We started to meet together across denominational boundaries, to worship and praise God and to listen to each other. We began to see His miracles of healing happen as we loved and respected each other in Him.

The Renewal transformed me. At last, I was finding the Church I had been looking for many years ago as a child. This was authentic, and I knew it deep down in my bones. I began to realise that we were all meant to do the things Jesus did by the same Holy Spirit through whom He did them on earth.

We were all in awe. However, we also were like children with new toys, and we made many mistakes through our over-enthusiasm, presumption, and lack of wise judgement. We had much to learn, but God had opened our eyes to possibilities far beyond our imaginings. His Word, the Bible, came alive for us. We began to pray in new ways. We began to expect to see God act and to heal and build people up. We slowly began to see that faith was not articles in a creed but a live force that, when used in obedience to God, would produce results. We began to listen, expectant that He would tell us what to do and He did! God smiled and was very patient, for we had to give up our old ways of thinking and learn how to live in a whole new way. Such a transition takes time, but as for me, I came alive! I had known the Father and Jesus most of my life, but I had no active experience of the Holy Spirit. (Why, we even called Him the Holy Ghost!)

The Holy Spirit enabled me to open myself up, to walk in the light with those in authority over me, and to pray in small groups spontaneously. How hard that was at first! I learnt to listen expectantly and obey His promptings. We all listened to guest speakers from other parts of the Body, and the barriers began to melt. It was a beginning. *I was glad when they said to me, Let us go to the Lord's house* (Ps. 122: 1). We could hardly wait for the next meeting. We all knew God was busy changing His Church.

He is renewing it again.

What was started then, God is building on today. We are in a fresh move of His Spirit. God is opening us up to new and exciting possibilities as He brings us into the kind of unity He desires, and that is essential for the times in which we are now living. *We need to remember the mistakes we made back then so that we do not make them this time.* Overenthusiasm needs to yield to humility. Our timing needs to yield to His perfect timing. After all, we are His servants. He is not our servant! Perseverance through the suffering that happens when we stand for Christ is a part of our refinement. This refinement by the Holy Spirit is necessary to build up the character of Christ in us, for it brings us into unity with Him. Holiness and commitment are necessary. Obedience is essential to His Spirit flowing, and freedom in the Spirit must be anchored in the truth of His word, the Bible. God is more concerned with our motivations than our performance. He is more interested that our security be in Him alone than in any other idol we put in His place. He wants His people passionate about His Son Jesus and focused on the establishment of His Kingdom. For all this to happen, He wants us in our prayer closets alone with Him, exploring the secrets of His presence and experiencing the wonders of His love. From the secret place with Him, He wants us to beam His love out to all the Church and the world. Imagine hundreds and thousands of spiritual radio stations (us) consistently beaming out waves of His love across the divides and into the darkest holes of evil in today's world. Nothing could withstand the impact of this. *It would cause a revolution in the spirit world.* Yet it takes every one of us to seek God in our own hearts consistently and be passionately committed to prayer in this way on a daily basis. It may be a quick arrow to heaven on a bus or train or thirty minutes in our quiet time or a night vigil in a hospital bed unable to sleep. If we all joined together, offering Him just that which we can give, He will take all this prayer and meld it as one with Jesus' prayer when He said, *I pray that they may all be one. Father! May they be in us, just as you are in me and I am in you. May they be one so that the world will believe that you sent me.*[34] The effect of this unity would be monumental. Prayer of this dimension produces results.

As a teenager, I saw this happen when Britain was fighting for its life in World War II. Our nation had no resources worth speaking about. But there was much prayer. After the war, I recall a Luftwaffe pilot giving his testimony of how he and his fellow pilots saw the Battle of Britain. He said, 'We were told Britain had no fighters, and so we came over very confident, with all our strength, to bomb them into surrender, but we were totally unprepared for all the planes that came at us from all directions. We realised we had been misinformed, and we retreated.' Other pilots saw huge balls of fire coming at them so that they became disoriented and lost control of their planes. Thank you, God, for answering prayer, for, practically speaking, we did not have those planes! *God answers prayer.*

Yes! There is a cost to all this. How much are we prepared to give Him? How much are we willing to let Him change us? Can we join Jesus in His prayer for the unity of love to flood this world? This is our chance, our time to live, and our opportunity to love in His way. Do we answer His call or not?

I am the Lord's servant, said Mary; *May it happen to me as you have said* (Luke 1: 38). Mary gave her consent, and the Son of God became man. God can do miracles with us too, if we will only give Him our consent!

Unity brings a healing balm just as division brings discord and friction. God has many ways of bringing healing to His world and very often He does this through His Church Body – us! He has been developing all of us our entire lives for the mission He designed for us to do. Long before He gave us the grace to accept His Son, He

---

[34] I pray not only for them, but also for those who believe in me because of their message. I pray that they may all be one. Father! May they be in us, just as you are in me and I am in you. May they be one, so that the world will believe that you sent me (John 17: 20–21).

had prepared good works for each of us to do,[35] works that will facilitate His Kingdom. He has used everything in our past to hone and mould us for our special assignment. Moses is an example. God gave him forty years of training in Pharaoh's court and then forty years of training in the desert before he was given his great commission to lead God's people out of Egypt, from slavery to the Promised Land. *So God was developing Moses for his assignment for eighty years!* God is not bothered by how old we are. He trains us and gives us the experience and the tools to do His job. I believe He trains every one of His children in this way. He certainly has me! All of us are equal in His sight, but our roles are different because His assignment is unique for each of us. We cannot be like another person. We are incredibly put together by God for a specific destiny.

The enemy has tried hard to remove God's concept of our identity from us. He has used pain inflicted on us by people to try to distort our visions, both of who God is and of how He sees us. Our own reactions to people have also, over time, hardened this wrong vision, so even we do not see ourselves as God created us to be. We settle for far less than God intends for us. We listen to the lies of satan and even start telling ourselves they are true, like Eve did. So we fall far short of the glorious person God created. He gave each of us some of His glory, but we have chosen to believe we are what our culture, our family, our education, and finally, we ourselves tell us we are. *Satan is delighted, because he knows that the way we see ourselves is the way we will act.*

He even tried this strategy on Jesus. You will remember that when Jesus was baptised in the Jordan by John the Baptist, the heavens opened. The Spirit descended as a dove and settled and remained on Jesus, and the Father's voice from heaven declared who Jesus was, *This is my own dear Son with whom I am pleased* (Matt. 3: 17). Immediately following this, Christ was led by the Holy Spirit into the desert and was tempted by the devil. *Why?* The first words the devil spoke tell us why. The devil said, *If you*

---

[35] God has made us what we are, and in our union with Christ Jesus he has created us for a life of good deeds, which he has already prepared for us to do (Eph. 2: 10).

are God's Son . . . (Luke 4: 3). He tried to put doubt into Jesus' mind that God had spoken the truth. Satan used the same strategy when he tempted Eve! But Jesus always counted on what God, His Father, spoke, and He dismissed satan after his third attempt at querying Jesus' identity. He does the same with us. If satan can convince us that we are not wonderfully and fearfully created by God for a divine purpose and if he can get us to believe we are less than we are, we will act this out in our lives, believing his lies and missing our unique role in God's great plan.

God said, *I chose you before I gave you life, and before you were born I selected you to be a prophet to the nations* (Jer. 1: 5). *God created us. He used our earthly parents.* They did not create us. Jesus paid an enormous price for us on the cross. The Holy Spirit can affect the wonderful transformation from how we see ourselves to how God sees us.

Graphic 10 - Our Covenant with Ourselves

If we continue to see ourselves as less than God sees us, we play into the enemy's hands. Very often, it is from this deception that we have got our distorted ideas of life and our purpose in it, even our identity!

This is the first healing we need, to believe and act in the truth that we are God's loving creation, not some fluke or accident of nature. Our identity is special, and when we start to believe that, many other things fall into place. Gratitude and wonder replace self-doubt and depression. We learn to dismiss satan's lies about us, and life takes on new meaning, for we want to fulfil our destiny and start living for and with God. This agreeing with God's purpose for our lives brings us into union with our first parent, God. We realise how much He loves us and how much He has done to prove it to us. Our hearts expand; our heads lift, and we understand that we want to thank and praise Him. Realisation leads us into spontaneous praise.

Coming into union with Him leads us to want to give out to others this glorious truth because He has not just done this for us, but He has made this knowledge available to the whole world. We want to give them the Good News. We want to join with other Christians who have now understood who they really are and the wondrous freedom that that brings. We want to share our good fortune, and that brings us into unity with those who are also walking in this truth. As we go together, we will meet the same opposition that Jesus coped with 2,000 years ago. It should not surprise us! But if we are together, we can overcome. We will remember that we too were blind until Jesus touched our eyes. As God had much patience with us, so too can we, with His grace, be patient with others. We can bring them friendship and walk with them in their moccasins for a mile or two, to understand their need and see how it can be best met. I love Saint Francis's prayer, which perhaps you know. He lived this way!

> Make me a channel of Your peace,
> Where there is hatred, let me sow Your love,
> Where there is injury, Your pardon, Lord,
> And where there's doubt, true faith in You.

O, Master, grant that I may never seek,
So much to be consoled as to console,
To be understood, as to understand,
To be loved as to love with all my soul.

Make me a channel of your peace,
Where there's despair in life, let me bring hope.
Where there is darkness, only light.
And where there's sadness, ever joy.

This hymn beautifully outlines the role of the Christian in this world. Jesus said that we were like the Light of the World. He told us to be as the Good Samaritan and care for people. As we went together in His name, He would be there with us to bring healing and deliverance, sight and hearing, and other miraculous happenings by His Holy Spirit actively manifesting the presence of God. Are we to expect to see such happenings when we pray? Yes, for He said we would.

Several years ago I went on a mission trip[36] to India, the land of my birth. There were thousands eagerly coming forward for prayer, so we could only spend a little time with each one. I saw in front of me an Indian lady whose eyeballs were up in her head so that only the white parts of her eyes were visible. She had been totally blind for fifteen years.

---

[36] This mission trip was organized by Harvest International Ministries led by Director Rev. Erik Tammaru. We were ministering to 1,000 Indian pastors who belong to HIM. HIM is a network of like-minded churches, ministries and missionaries committed to loving and helping each other fulfill the Great Commission. It has more than 20 thousand churches in over 50 nations and on 5 continents affiliated with it. The senior pastors are Reverends Che and Sue Ahn. The mother church is situated in Ambassador Auditorium, Pasadena, California, USA. It was an honour to be a part of this outreach.

Graphic 11 - Healing in India

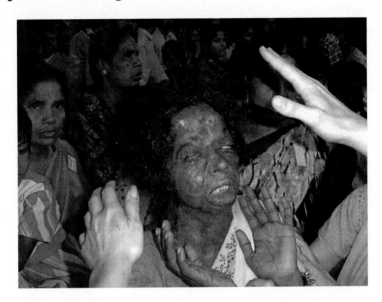

I prayed and moved on. I looked back to find other members of our team praying over her too. Then it happened right before our eyes – her eyes came down! She had a nasty cataract obliterating her vision in her left eye, but her right eye was now normal and she could see clearly!

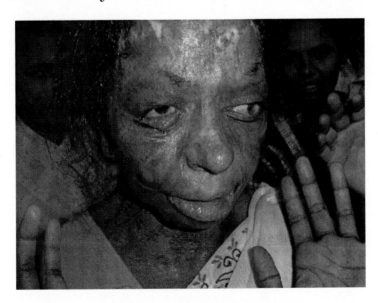

I also saw a little boy, aged about eight, who we were told had never walked and had to be carried everywhere. As prayer and encouragement were ministered to him, this young boy took his first steps into his father's arms. There was much rejoicing!

Is it only in Third World countries that this is happening? No!

In the ministry of Resurrected Life, to which God has called me, I see miracles of grace happening in people's lives almost daily. Testimonies are powerful and confirm that God is healing and restoring His Body right here in our midst. Here are a few samples: there are so many; it is hard to choose!

These testimonies are from people belonging to different ethnic groups and different Church affiliations.

'This class saved my marriage. The Lord fulfilled me so much that I started loving my husband without resentment. This ministry also helped me to restore my identity as God's child and as a woman. I enjoy this ministry so much that I feel a calling to receive more training in order to help others.'

'I have been blessed by the healing power of Christ inside and out. It feels like fresh water was poured in. Yes, I feel more loved. I feel like I have family.'

'My understanding of being born again into the Kingdom has greatly enhanced. My understanding of how the Holy Spirit moves has been enlarged. My ability to counter the lies of the adversary with God's truth has helped me to move into a new area of understanding and in turn to use this to bless my family.'

'The Word that was presented was so good. The class helped me realise what God has to say about me. I learnt how God wants me to think and live and that he wants me to be free.'

'I love the class. I feel like a close family! Molly, you have opened my life to Jesus. Thanks.'

'One year ago, I came to the first RLM class hopeless, suicidal, and desperately fearful about everything. To the glory of God, He has become the total answer for all of life.'

'I have experienced ministry and inner healing and deliverance. Life is better in every way.'

'Everything God promises He delivers and more. Resurrected Life can come alive in each one of us. It is a journey least travelled. Chains will fall, hearts will be healed, and minds renewed. I am humbled to be a small part of this ministry.'

'Having experienced the shallow depths of New Age, my life started to be "switched on" the moment I entered into the house of Resurrected Life Ministries. Within seven days, my worldview began to change. God spoke clearly to me regarding my future and old bondages, and generational curses were broken and vanished. I am free. I love it. I breathe it and teach it. God bless you abundantly.'

'I was involved in so many things like drugs, drink, and women, but my life was a mess. The class has opened my eyes to see that God can take care of my past and still bring me to a new place where I can fulfil my real destiny. I never realised God's love for me before. Thank you.'

Testimonies from Korea

'My circumstances are not changed, but I choose to love me in the way God sees me. I understand that it does not happen through my effort or by what I do. I nail my self-righteousness to the cross and trust God to change me. I am out of the cage now and have faith that He will hold me and teach me to fly.'

'In the class I meet myself, in faith I walk through the cross and leave fear, diligence, blame, anger, rage, bitterness, brawling, slander, and malice on the cross as I choose to live with Him. I repent that I have lived in the natural and choose to live now in the supernatural.'

'Through the teaching God reveals to me what bondages I was bound and what was hidden deep inside of me. During the ministry, God reveals to me how much He loves me and considers me most valuable. Now I begin and end each day with thanksgiving.'

In our ministry, our signature tune is, 'Bind us together with cords that cannot be broken, Bind us together, Lord, bind us together with love.' And He does! Resurrected Life is just one of the many ways God is healing and building His people up together to belong to His end-time army against satan. It is such a joy to be a part of it! It is thrilling to be moving in the same way, towards the same goal.

I have found, through ministering God's Love to thousands of Christians, that there are *two major pitfalls* blocking the Love of God from flowing powerfully through Christians who have turned away from sin.

1. *Many do not know who they are now that their sins have been washed away.* They do not see themselves as wonderful creations of a generous God or as His delightful children. They need to change their glasses to God's glasses and start acting in their new God-given identities in Christ.
2. *Because they do not see who they are, they do not act in the supernatural life they have been given.* They still try to tackle life from the natural vantage point, using natural tools, which do not work spiritually. God is Spirit, and we are spirits, created and now regenerated in Jesus. We have a supernatural life by which all natural problems can be tackled. But we do not act this way. *Instead, we keep trying to do spiritual deeds with natural weapons and we fail.* It cannot be done that way! Meanwhile, the devil is delighted to see us fail. This does not honour God our Father.

However, Christians who know who they are and act in the authority and power they have been given, obedient to their Father in heaven, are a power that will shake and destroy evil. Satan backs away in fear, for Jesus leads such a group. When we have many such groups joined together in His love, we see the Church He came to enable us to arise healthy, ardent, and strong in unity with Him.

Where Jesus is, there is unity, healing, and love. There is direction and focus, obedience and perfect trust in our leader. Let us give Him the reins of our lives. Let us give Him the reins of His Church. He is *the* Lord. Let us rejoice together in the wonder of Jesus' love as the Holy Spirit fulfils the mighty plan of God. What an awesome Trinity they are!

CHAPTER 6

Unity with Our Past – Our Heritage

(I am indebted to Diana Chapman for her book *Britain's Spiritual Inheritance* for some of the information in this chapter.)

Unity is an absolute essential for continuance for as Scripture tells us, *A house divided against itself will not stand* (Mark 3: 25). In the earliest days of the Church, believers saw the need for a creed that would succinctly encapsulate the foundational beliefs to which all Christians could agree and adhere to . . . a framework of faith. It is thought that the *Apostles' Creed*, stemming from the first or second century, gave this foundation. It is still used today, so I quote the ecumenical version of the English Language Liturgical Consultation (ELLC).

I believe in God, the Father almighty,
Creator of heaven and earth.
I believe in Jesus Christ, God's only Son, our Lord,
who was conceived by the Holy Spirit,
born of the Virgin Mary,
suffered under Pontius Pilate,
was crucified, died, and was buried;
He descended to the dead.
On the third day He rose again;
He ascended into heaven,
He is seated at the right hand of the Father,

66

and He will come to judge the living and the dead.
I believe in the Holy Spirit,
the holy Catholic Church,
the communion of saints,
the forgiveness of sins,
the resurrection of the body,
and the life everlasting. Amen.

I have highlighted the Communion of saints to show that this has always been a firm belief for all Christians, for we are all called to unity in Christ. It has always been and will always continue to be that our unity in Him is what makes us belong to the great family of God. It is the Holy Spirit who is the unity of the Father and Son, Who also binds us together into unity with God. We have brothers and sisters all over the world today *and* throughout the centuries. Thus, it is good to recognise and praise God for those who have gone before us. They in their turn kept the faith and passed it on to us. We in our turn are responsible to keep the torch of faith burning brightly and pass it on to future generations.

So how has the Holy Spirit empowered our ancestors, some of whom have given their lives rather than deny this faith? Who are these people to whom we owe so much? In this quick flit through our history, we can only highlight a few, but let us be eternally grateful for the many that are only known to God, but who because of the communion of saints we may one day meet in eternity.

Living in the present is a very good way to live, but we do need to remember all that has happened to make our present possible. As Christians, where we are today is very dependent on what has happened in the past. In this chapter, I am speaking here of our past in Britain, for you the reader, there will be other names and outpourings of God's grace relevant to your own cultural heritage.

With this in mind, let us explore with gratitude our British Christian heritage. There is a wonderful awareness of unity when we do, for we are one family – God's great family past and present. I will be including some of the moves of God that happened elsewhere but which have had a profound effect on us here in Britain.

Our first thousand years

It all started for us in Britain when Julius Caesar, way back in BC 35, sent explorers to set up a trade relationship with our ancestors. Then Claudius Caesar in AD 33 (the same year that Jesus died) established Britain as a Roman province. Stories of Jesus were told by Roman soldiers and the traders who came, thus preparing the way for the Truth to penetrate Britain.

Here I am quoting some information from Google that has astonished me – perhaps it will astonish you too.

'The Christian religion began in Britain within fifty years of Christ's ascension,' writes Robert Parsons, the Jesuit, in his *Three conversions of England*. The venerable Bede writing about AD 740 mentions, 'The Britons preserved the Faith which they received under legendary King Lucius (140) uncorrupted and continued in peace and tranquillity until the time of the Emperor Diocletian.'[37]

Also, Gildas the Wise, a Welsh monk and historian (425–512), distinctly says that the light of Christ shone here in Britain in the last years of the emperor Tiberius Caesar (AD 14–37).[38]

So there is much documentation that supports the early beginnings of our Christian heritage.

Following the terrible persecutions of Christians by Diocletian (283–305), the emperor Constantine in AD 324 stopped all persecution and freed people to live as Christians openly. He did not realise that his well-meaning act would allow the floodgates of nominality into the Church – people called themselves Christian without any inner conviction of the truth. Satan had changed

---

[37] *http://asis.com/users/stag/glastonb.html*

[38] Gildas, *De Exidio Brittaniae*, Sec. 8, p.25, AD 550, quoted in http:// *www. goodshepherdaoc* /Anglican/Traditional.html

his attack. He could not stamp out the Church from without, so he changed to polluting Christian belief from within. For many centuries to our present day, satan divides the Church through disagreement in what we believe. Hence, the many segments of Church there are today. To counter this, the Church came together in several councils to sort out authentic doctrine and keep united (e.g. AD 313 the council of Arles to which Britain sent three bishops to represent us).[39]

The Romans finally left Britain in 412, and we were invaded by the Saxons, the Angles, and the Jutes, all of whom brought with them their own gods, and inevitably, this caused a dilution of faith as mixed marriages took place. Yet somehow Christianity survived on the Western edges of Britain. Missionary activity continued in Wales and Ireland, and in western Scotland, Saint Columba helped to bring a distinctly Irish brand of Christianity to mainland Britain.[40]

In AD 420, Pope Leo sent missionaries to re-evangelise us. This they did evidencing the truth through miracles just like Jesus had done.

God used several ways to keep the Church advancing. He still does today.

A. He used kings and queens throughout many centuries.
B. He used the clergy who worked in parishes or communities, and also the monks and nuns who showed by their dedicated lives the truth of the Gospel.
C. He singled out individuals and anointed them most wonderfully to spread the Good News.

Let me give examples of these in three ways:

A)
1) **King Lucius** (thought to be a legendary king possibly AD 85–150)

---

[39] http://www.christianitytoday.com/ch/asktheexpert/aug22.html
[40] http://www.bbc.co.uk/religion/religions/Christianity/history/uk_1.shtml

It has been recorded by Bede and others that legendary king Lucius, when king of Britain, wrote to the Pope (Eleutherius) and asked for baptism to become a Christian in 140. This was granted, and the king reportedly founded several churches including the cathedral in London. It was thought he was the first Christian King in Britain.[41]

2) **King Alfred the Great** (846–901)

He and his grandson Athelstan did much to repel the Vikings, who brought with them foreign gods.

'An aura of religious significance surrounded these events. For the Christian Anglo-Saxons, the defining characteristic of the Viking invaders was their paganism. In the late ninth century, when the Christian kingdoms of England faced annihilation, notions of Christian service and sacrifice crystallised with the heroic tradition expressed in such Old English poems as Beowulf to form a new heroic ideal. In the tenth century, the new ethos of Christian heroism was employed to great effect by the West Saxon kings in their creation of a unified kingdom of England.'[42]

3) **King Edward I** (1003–1066)

King Edward I had considerable healing gifts, and many miracles are reported in his reign.

B) Saint Augustine and Saint Benedict who founded the Augustinians and Benedictines, respectively

Saint Augustine wrote his rule for monastic communal living in 397. He taught that nothing conquers except truth, and the fruit of truth is love. 'Let all of you then live together, one in mind and heart, mutually giving honour to God in yourselves, whose temples you have become' (The Rule of Augustine of Hippo).[43] His friars were trained to do evangelism among the poor with whom

---

[41] http://en.wikipedia.org/wiki/Lucius_of_Britain

[42] www.heroicage.org/issues/7/hare.html

[43] http://www.augnet.org/?ipageid=266

they lived and to teach both in parishes and universities that God's way of living, as evidenced in Jesus' life, was a far better way than following the maxims of the world. His rule spread to many communities across the continent and to Britain. There are in the world today over 2,000 monks (not including the nuns) who follow Augustine's rule. Here in England, many different orders follow the Augustinian rule. I belonged to one and was trained in this way for six years. (We nursed the sick in city slums.)

Benedict (480–543) defined a monastery as a 'school for the service of the Lord'. He composed a rule of life which balanced prayer, liturgical celebration of the Psalms, divided into seven daily sessions which were often chanted together, manual labour, (he said 'to labour is to pray') and time for study.[44] This blueprint became the model on which most monastic life was built. Many Christian priests privately follow this plan as a daily practice today. In those days, monasteries often became the centres of community life, providing a farm, hospital, inn for travellers, a school, and a library. They were also places of refuge and healing where miracles regularly occurred.

In 2008, there were over 25,000 Benedictines in fifty countries that abide by this rule of life. (In Britain alone, there are several hundred Benedictine monks and 300 nuns today. Some Benedictine congregations today are Worth Abbey in Sussex, Douai, Downside, Buckfast, Ampleforth, and others.)[45]

C) God's anointed individual

Patrick, in *432*, was born somewhere on the west coast of Britain. He was captured by pirates and taken to Ireland and sold to a druid lord. But he escaped, and through many adventures, he converted much of Ireland to Christ and founded many churches there.[46]

It is amazing what God does when people are willing!

---

[44] http://www.middle-ages.org.uk/benedictine-monks.htm

[45] Ref://http://www.benedictines.org.uk/maps.htm

[46] Saint Patrick – Christian Classics Ethereal Library, http.//www.ccel.org/ccel/Patrick

In 597, Pope Gregory sent Augustine of Canterbury and forty monks to England to re-evangelise us because through the Angles invading Britain we were in danger of losing the faith.[47]

In *616,* Paulinus, an Augustinian monk, was sent north from Kent to ensure that Ethelburga, a Christian princess, would be allowed to practise her faith married to King Edwin, the pagan king of Northumbria. Through Paulinus, both he and many of his court became Christian. Paulinus was the first archbishop of York.[48]

God used both the Roman brand from Kent and the Celtic brand of Christianity from Ireland to evangelise Northumbria. Paulinus was from Kent, and Aidan (born around 590 – 651) from Lindisfarne, a monastic community that had originally come from Ireland. Aidan would walk for miles talking happily to everyone and converting as he went. He was very successful in bringing many to Christ.[49]

Saint Patrick, Saint Columba, and Saint Aidan were all well-known for the healings and miracles that accompanied their preaching.

In *633,* Pope Honorius sent Birinus to evangelise Britain. The Popes were very instrumental in ensuring that Britain remained Christian. Birinus, a Frank, founded many churches in Wessex and beyond, such as Saint Mary's of Reading or Saint Helen's of Abingdon. He converted the West Saxon king and his family and was given Dorchester to be his bishopric.[50]

In *635,* there were two streams of Christianity in Britain, the Celtic and the Roman, and it was thought wise to come together, so in *644,* under (a woman) Hilda the wise, a meeting was called at Whitby. It was agreed that an English Church be governed from the Archbishoprics of Canterbury and York, but in matters of theology, Church architecture, and the monasteries, the English Church would be guided by the wider Christian Church-body.

---

[47] http://www.bbc.co.uk/religion/religions/Christianity/history/uk_1.shtml

[48] http://Justus.anglican.org/resources/bio/263.html

[49] http://webspace.webring.com/people/ee/essentials1/

[50] http://en.wikipedia.org/wiki/Birinus

Celtic Christianity was pushed to the western margins of Britain.[51]

In the seventh century, Britain was called the Isle of the Saints for Christianity flourished. It produced Saint Patrick, Saint Ninian of Scotland, Saint David in Wales and many others[52] – but then the Vikings attacked in 871, and this caused many to be martyred and much disruption to many communities. However, King Alfred, the Christian king of Wessex, defeated the Vikings at Eddington and set up schools with the idea of having Christianity capturing the imagination of ordinary illiterate country people.

In the tenth century, lords began to provide small chapels on their land where local people could use the services of a priest. This sowed the seeds of the parish system, still in existence today.[53]

We owe so much to these wonderful people who paved the way for what we can so easily take for granted. This is a quick summary of how Christianity came and spread in the first thousand years in Britain. Now we will look at the second millennium and see what happened.

The second thousand years

King Edward the Confessor (1042–1066) was brought up in Normandy. He was devoutly Christian and was blessed by the Pope. He instituted a royal practice that lasted until 1712, by which the ruling monarch would pray for those suffering from skin diseases, especially of the head and neck. The king would touch their heads saying, 'The King touches you, the Lord heals you.' Many miracles have been recorded of those healed. In only one year, he prayed for over a thousand people. King Edward

---

[51] Diana Chapman, *Britain's Spiritual Inheritance*, p.40, ISBN: 978-1-908393-23-4.

[52] Diana Chapman, *Britain's Spiritual Inheritance*, p.36.

[53] http://www.bbc.co.uk/religion/religions/christianity/history/uk_1.shtml

commissioned the building of Westminster Abbey, in which he is buried.[54]

The Norman Invasion

One date that gets implanted into every British child's mind in school, and which they do not usually forget, is *1066*. There was a big battle at Hastings, and we were defeated by a Norman duke, William the conqueror, who was crowned king of England on Christmas day. This set up years of conflict between France and England because William, as a duke, was under the king of France, yet was king of England. He soon conquered all of Britain and brought us closer to the continent by introducing some of his French cultural ways. William supported the monastic and parish systems already flourishing and did much to build roads and townships with the Church as the ruling power.[55]

Saint Bernard (1090–1153)

Much of the known world was sunk deep into selfishness. It affected the Church as well as the lives of ordinary people. Spirituality was at an all-time low. God anointed a young nobleman to seek a higher chivalry, to give his whole life to God for God to do with it as He liked. He was drawn into the monastery of Citeaux in France, the Cistercians, and he brought with him thirty members of his family (1112).[56] Stephen Harding, an Englishman, was his superior, and Bernard made such progress that he was sent to found a new monastery at Clairvaux. Young men flocked to join, and soon, there were 300 men wanting a better life. Sixty-five new monasteries were founded, and Bernard grew into a gifted spiritual writer who had a real influence on those in authority outside of the monastery. He did much to

---

[54] Diana Chapman, *Britain's Spiritual Inheritance*, p.109.

[55] *http://www.historyguy.com/norman_conquest_england.html*

[56] www.christianitytoday.com/ch/131christians/moversandshakers/bernard clairvaux

reconcile England and France and helped to solve the schism that had erupted in the papacy.

There were eighty-five such monasteries in Britain at this time, filled with ardent young men seeking God with their whole heart. This had a great impact spiritually and raised people's desire to fulfil their lives as God wanted.

It was a monastic era because just around the corner came Saint Francis and Saint Dominic, who both spent their lives evangelising the poor and downtrodden.[57]

Saint Dominic (1170–1221)

Born in Spain, he became a priest at twenty-five and spent ten years studying theology and living under the Augustinian rule. His bishop asked him to come to France with him. They spent the night in an inn whose landlord was an Albigentian, a heresy rampant at that time throughout Christendom, which taught that all matter was sinful and so advocated severity to the body (dying of starvation was considered holy!). Dominic spent the whole night enlightening this man and realised he was being called to help ordinary people to understand the true Gospel. He got papal authority to found an order of trained men who could evangelise well. They were called Black Friars as they wore a white habit and black cloak. In 2010, there were 5,900 Black Friars in the world doing this work.[58] My own husband was instructed by one in Oxford prior to our marriage.

Saint Francis of Assisi (1182–1226)

While attending Mass, the words of Scripture telling us to go out and preach the Gospel to all hit Francis as a call by God. He dedicated his life to follow this call. Pope Innocent III commissioned him to follow a very simple lifestyle – owning nothing, walking among the poor, and bringing healing and help to those lost in the world's selfish schemes. Francis and his

---

[57] *http://www.bbc.co.uk/religions/christianity/history/uk*

[58] *http://en.wikipedia.org/wiki/Dominican_Order*

followers worked for their food and showed by their example how to live pure and holy lives. Many joined Francis, giving up everything to follow Jesus' way as closely as possible. He helped Clare to found the order of contemplative sisters (the Poor Clares) who supported the friars in prayer both then and now. Francis went to the Holy Land to try to convert the Muslim leaders to stop the conflict which was causing the crusades. However, those in his own order were in disagreement at home, so he returned and resigned from leadership in order to finish writing the rule for his third order of lay missionaries.[59]

There are many Franciscans in Britain and all over the world today – they are much loved. I served as head of a Franciscan primary school for twelve years in Ascot, England. They were good years!

Juliana of Norwich (born in 1342)

It is thought that she was a Benedictine nun, living as a recluse in an anchorage, part of which still remains in the churchyard of Saint Julian of Norwich which belongs to the Carrow Priory. When she was thirty years old, she received a revelation of God's divine love for people that stayed with her all her life. She wrote, when she was able, some of this wonder in 'Sixteen Revelations of Divine Love', extracts of which are in the British museum. She showed clearly the unity between our souls and our bodies that were both created in His love. She taught that knowing God went hand in hand with knowing oneself. While contemplating the crucifix, she was drawn by God into the sufferings of Christ. With this illumination, the whole mystery of Redemption and the purpose of human life became clear to her. Even the possibility of sin and the existence of evil did not trouble her because *she saw that it will all be swept away by the 'bliss of love. This is the great deed, transcending our reason, that the Blessed Trinity shall do at the last day.'* So she councils, *'let nothing disturb thee, let nothing affright thee, God is over all.'*[60]

---

[59] *http://www.fordham.edu/halsall/source/stfran-rule.html*
[60] http://www.newadvent.org/cathen/08557a.htm

John Wycliffe (1329–1384)

John was an Oxford scholar and, together with those around him, was responsible for translating the Bible into English for all to read. With this translation, he and his followers (called the Lollards) went to any who would listen, proclaiming the truth of the Gospels. They challenged some of the Church practices of the day and so came in for some persecution. Nevertheless, their work sowed in England and Scotland the seeds of the Reformation. It pointed to the Biblical text and gave ordinary people the chance to read Scripture in their own language, so it encouraged lay folk to learn to read.[61]

William Caxton, in 1476, *set up the first printing press in Britain.* Books became more easily available for the general public, especially the Bible.

From the fourteenth Century to the twenty-first century, there have been many outpourings of grace that have kept the faith alive, but in the space I have, it is impossible to speak of all, so I must select.

Martin Luther (1483–1546)

Martin Luther (1483–1546) was an Augustinian monk who was seeking God with all his heart. God gave him a revelation of the wonder of faith by grace, whereas the Church of his day was focused on working our way to heaven. Inevitably, a clash ensued. Luther pointed out many ways (his ninety-six theses) that the Church was off track, and naturally, this did not go down well with those in authority. Luther was eventually excommunicated from the Catholic Church and thus began the separation of those that followed Rome and those that protested against the corrupt practices of Rome. Thus, they were called Protestants and were persecuted for their stand. Luther was right, and only recently, Pope John Paul II agreed with him and repented publically on

---

[61] *http://www.middle-ages.org.uk/john-wycliffe.htm*

behalf of the Catholic Church for the way Luther had been treated – stating that if he had been born in a different era, Martin Luther would likely have been hailed as a doctor in the Church. Luther said, 'At last meditating day and night, by the mercy of God, I began to understand that the righteousness of God is that through which the righteous live by a gift of God, namely by faith. Here I felt as if I had been entirely born again and had entered paradise itself through the gates that had been flung open.'[62]

The English Reformation

King Henry VIII (1491–1547) is a well-known figure in English history. He developed the Royal Navy, increasing the ships from five to fifty-five and equipped them with guns. Henry wanted a male heir to succeed him, but both his sons died. That is why he sought the Pope for an annulment so he could remarry. The Pope refused because in Catholic eyes marriage is indissoluble. Henry asked the Archbishop of Canterbury to grant him his divorce against Catholic teaching and to curry favour with the King, the archbishop agreed. Henry declared himself head of the Church in England and divorced both his wife and the English Church from Rome. There was no outcry against this because the poor, at that time, were being oppressed by the clergy who demanded money for performing marriages, infant baptisms, and death ceremonies. The monasteries had become decadent and rich and so Henry in his new role sent his viceroy Oliver Cromwell to destroy the monasteries and seize their wealth. The Pope excommunicated Henry, who went on to marry several young women who failed to have a male child that lived to maturity. His oldest daughter Mary was Queen from 1553 to 1558, and when she died, Elizabeth, his second daughter, became Queen (1558–1603). Henry kept the Latin liturgical language, which later became abandoned for the English version. Thus, the Church of England became separated from Catholic Christianity. People's loyalties were put to the test, and this led to many martyrdoms on both sides in the succeeding years.[63]

---

[62] http://www.christianitytoday.com/ch/131christians/theologians/luther.html
[63] *http://www.royal.gov.uk/history*ofthemonarchy/kingsandqueensofengland/t . . .

The way we look at history matters. Many of us have been taught to see in a certain sectarian way, for example Protestant or Catholic, but God has shown us clearly that He uses both to extend his Kingdom. *This has been delightfully expressed by Diana Chapman in her book, Britain's Spiritual Inheritance,* from which I now quote:

'If you think about any river, it has a source. All rivers begin as springs from underground, and as they bubble up, they are fed by numerous tributaries and swollen by rainfall. If you trace this scenario back to the beginning, all the water they contain came from the same source, rain. Some has just been stored millions of years in underground chambers or rivers.

'So the rivers of different denominations ultimately have the source of their life in heaven. Rather than see denominations as sectarian strongholds, let's see them as historical manifestations of the work of the Holy Spirit in the earth and celebrate their creativity and diversity.

'It's easy to write of denominations as divisive, but when you begin to explore their beginnings, you find that many were born in revival or centred around a newly discovered truth. Frequently, there was a charismatic figure or group whose heart beat with heaven. It's just that what was bubbling in them couldn't be contained in the existing Church structures (p. 44)'[64] – Exactly!

The Puritans (1564–1660)

As so often happens, those within the new Church of England became lax spiritually, and so reform was in the air again. C. S. Lewis is reported to have said, 'These Puritans were young bucks who wanted to go all the way with God and the Bible.' They worked towards religious, moral, and social reforms. The writings and ideas of *John Calvin*, a leader in the Reformation, gave rise to Protestantism and were pivotal in the Christian revolt. The Puritans were one branch of dissenters who decided that the Church of England was beyond reform. Escaping persecution

---

[64] Diana Chapman, *Britain's Spiritual Inheritance*, p.44.

from Church leadership and the king, they sailed away on the Mayflower to America in 1620.

Reaction to Catholic ways of worship caused groups within the Puritans to split – those who opted for retaining bishops (Anglican version), those who dispensed with bishops (Presbyteran version), and those who opted for complete self-governing churches (Congregationist version). Almost all the Puritan clergy left the Church of England in 1660, some becoming non-conformist ministers. Great emphasis was placed on educating their young people who were encouraged to read their Bibles. For the first time in history, they organised free schools for children.[65]

Thomas Helwys, in 1611, led a small group from Amsterdam who there formed themselves into a Separatist Church under the leadership of John Smyth and practiced believer's baptism. Helwys was the author of *The Mystery of Iniquity*, the first English printed book to plead for full religious freedom. The successors of Helwys and his friends became known as General *Baptists*, and in 1633, a Calvinistic Separatist Church in London broke away from its brothers on adopting believer's baptism. They were called the Particular Baptists. Baptist churches were founded in Wales and Ireland in the mid seventeenth century and in Scotland by the mid-eighteenth century. They were and still are very strongly Bible-based.[66]

The Presbyterian Church of Scotland was first organised by *John Knox (mid-1500s)* and adopted as the national Church of Scotland in 1690. There have been many splits within the Church in later years, but it is still considered the National Church of Scotland.[67]

---

[65] http://www3.nd.edu/~rbarger/www7/puritans.html

[66] www.londonbaptistorg.uk/about-us/baptists/history-of-uk-baptists/

[67] http://christianity.about.com/od/presbyteriandenomination/a/presbyhistory.html

The Quakers

George Fox (1624–1691) began a four-year journey seeking answers to his spiritual questions. Disappointed with the answers he got from religious leaders, he sought God direct. ('Ask and you will receive.') Fox felt an inner calling to become an itinerant preacher. His meetings were radically different from orthodox Christianity and involved silent meditation, with no music or creeds or rituals. Soon, he had a following as more people began to listen to God direct. He taught that both men and women could hear God for themselves in this way. 'It was essentially the rediscovery by men and women whose whole training had been puritan of the mystical element which lies close to the heart of Christianity, but which puritanism, with all its strength, had strangely missed. It was a revivified consciousness of God, bringing with it the conviction that the essence of Christ's religion is not to be found in submission to outward authority, whether of Church or of the Bible, but in a direct experience of God in the soul and in a life lived in obedience to his will inwardly revealed.'[68]

By the seventeenth century, there were 15,000 Quakers in prison for their faith. Many were martyred and their children sent into slavery. But they survived, and there are many Quakers in the world today.

God was clearly showing through his people that it was possible to have an intimate personal relationship with Him. So I am including four Carmelites from this era who evidenced the same. Their writings are bestsellers to this day and have done much to help us all explore the wonder of personal relationship with God.

God's new emphasis on personal relationship

Brother Lawrence (1616–1691) was a Carmelite brother who actually spent most of his life working hidden in the monastic kitchen in Lorraine, France. His writing on *The Practice of the Presence of God* was published after his death and is even today

---

[68] www.bartleby.com/218/0401.html

regarded as a spiritual classic. It showed clearly that this personal, deep relationship with God is possible for everyone. 'In very truth we can render to God no greater or more signal proofs of our trust and faithfulness than by thus turning from things created to find our joy, though for a single moment, in the Creator . . . it is a common error among religious persons to neglect this practice of ceasing for a time that, which they are engaged upon, to worship God in the depth of their soul and to enjoy the peace of brief communion with Him.'[69]

The written word was now having a greater influence from other countries at this time and spiritual thought was spread in this way.

Other Carmelites such as *Saint John of the Cross (1542–1591)* and *Teresa of Avila (1515–1582)* were writing and advocating a concentration on the 'Interior Life' that we are all called to live. (Their writings became spiritual classics.) Then, later, the value of our inner life with God was demonstrated through the life of another Carmelite sister, *Saint Teresa of Lisieux (1873–1897)*. She lived her hidden life in a Carmelite convent and died at only twenty-six, yet the 'Little Way' she left us of how anyone could live close to God in a wonderful, personal way has affected many, many lives throughout Christianity today.

Surely God was showing us that inner transformation is what He desires for us, not mere conformity to a certain way of exterior worship.

This relationship caused outreach

He was also showing us that a life dedicated and obedient to Him can achieve much in this world.

a. *William Carey* (1761–1834) is a wonderful example of this. He was a cobbler in the north of England when he felt the call of God to go to India. It is quite amazing to read his life there and what was achieved (e.g. Timothy George, *The*

---

[69] Brother Lawrence, *The Practice of the Presence of God with Spiritual Maxims*, p. 72, ISBN: 0-8007-8599-1.

Life and Mission of William Carey, IVP). Through his life and preaching, many were converted, but he did not stop there. Through him the practice of sati was stopped (the ritual burning of young wives when their husbands died). He translated the Bible into Bengali, Sanskrit, and numerous other languages and dialects and taught the Indians how to make trains for travel and how to grow crops and timber that would help them live better lives and much more. He founded the first missionary society in 1792 and is known as the 'father of modern missions'.[70]

John Wesley (1703–1791) *is also an amazing example of what one man can do when on fire for God.* How did this happen? In 1735, as a young minister, he was aboard a ship headed from England to America; a storm arose, and even the captain feared for his life. However, John noticed a group of Moravian Christians singing hymns, and they were unafraid. After the storm had subsided, he asked them why they were not afraid? The Moravian leader responded with a question. 'Did he, Wesley, have faith in Christ?' This led to a time of soul-searching, and he realised that he did not trust Christ. As he put it, 'I was indeed fighting continually, but not conquering. . . I fell and rose and fell again.' However, on 24 May 1738, he had an experience. While someone was reading from Luther's writings about 'the change God works in the heart through faith in Christ, I felt my heart was strangely warmed. I felt I did trust in Christ, Christ alone for salvation, and an assurance was given to me that he had taken away my sins, even mine, and saved me from the law of sin and death.'

Meanwhile, *George Whitfield*, a friend and co-worker of Wesley, was having huge success seeing hundreds come to Christ in Bristol among the working-class poor, oppressed by industrialising England and neglected by the Church. So many were converting under his fiery preaching that he called on Wesley to help him.

---

[70] www.en.wikipedia.org/wiki/William_Carey_(missionary)

Later, Wesley travelled the length and breadth of England on horseback, preaching the Kingdom of God wherever he went. He started small groups of those wanting a closer walk with God and taught them his method, which later became known as *Methodism*. Through open confession of sin, people knew the freedom of relationship with God, and they would meet regularly to pray, study Scripture, and encourage each other to go deeper with God. The Methodists started schools and dispensaries for medicine. Wesley taught inner transformation leading to outward good works. He wrote many hymns which his brother Charles (1707–1788) put to music. Between them, they left us a heritage of worship that is sung in many lands today.[71]

The eighteenth century was turbulent. There were the French Revolution (1789–1799) and the Napoleonic wars (1803–1815), when Napoleon invaded Italy and took the Pope captive to France where he was kept for six months and died. There followed a resurgence of Catholicism in Europe, while in America the First Great Awakening (1730–1760) and the Second Awakening (1790–1840) were boosting the Evangelistic way of thought. Britain was affected by both.

The age of tolerance was birthed and with it much doubt about some fundamentals of our Christian faith. In the Church of England, three sections appeared: High Church similar to the Catholic way, Liberal Church, and Low Evangelical Church. It still calls itself a Church for everyone.

We were becoming much more aware that we were a part of a greater world, rather than a separatist island secure in our independence. So also, the sending of missionaries multiplied across the denominations. To convert the heathen in continents that did not know Christ became our focus. *In the nineteenth century and early twentieth century,* there came a switch in our thinking from bettering lives in this world to peopling heaven. There was a world focus on evangelising the lost.

---

[71] http://www.christianitytoday.com/ch/131christians/denominational founders. . .

David Livingstone (1813–1873) was one of the best-known missionaries in Victorian Britain. He was a student at Charing Cross Hospital, where he studied medical practices, midwifery, and botany from 1838 to 1840. Later, he went as a protestant missionary to Africa. He had a way of reassuring chiefs, preaching a Christian message, while respecting their tribal ways. He went where no missionary had ever been and was one of the first men to cross Africa.[72]

William Wilberforce (1847–1853) and *Lord Salisbury* were Christian politicians who broke the terrible curse of slavery that was such a source of revenue here in Britain. After his conversion to evangelical Christianity, William gave up his former life of racehorse gambling and devoted his energies to take up the cause against slavery in Parliament. He spent many years fighting fierce opposition and saw the abolition of slavery bill passed on 26 July 1833, only three days before he died.[73] Lord Salisbury also worked tirelessly on improving conditions of British factory workers and prisons as well as the education system for the poor.

Elizabeth Fry (1780–1845) was a Quaker who campaigned for prison reform and was invited to speak in the house of Lords where she taught that it was only the truths of the Gospel that could change the human heart. Queen Victoria was one of her admirers. In 1817, she helped to found the *Association for the Reformation of Female Prisoners in Newgate,* which became the first nationwide women's organisation in Britain. Then in 1840, she opened a training school for nurses. Her programme inspired Florence Nightingale, who took some of these nurses to help wounded soldiers in the Crimean war. Elizabeth Fry married and had eleven children as well![74]

William Booth (1829–1912), at thirteen, was apprenticed to a pawnbroker and two years later was converted to Methodism. After his apprenticeship ended, he was unemployed, so he read extensively and became a lay preacher and moved to London.

---

[72] http://en.wikipedia.org/wiki/David_Livingstone
[73] http://abolition.e2bn.org/people_24.html
[74] http://en.wikipedia.org/wiki/Elizabeth_Fry

Here he found his destiny which was to bring the Good News to the destitute in London. He founded the Christian Mission which became the *Salvation Army* in 1878, known for its self-sacrificing Christian social work such as soup kitchens and humanitarian aid in its many forms. Only two years later, this spread to America and many other countries under the British Empire where the Salvation Army still flourishes today.[75]

Diana Chapman writes, 'The 1880s were the "Healing Decade" for Britain . . . In London a healing home called Bethshan had been opened in 1865 by American holiness teacher W. E. Boardman, although the Quaker Elizabeth Baxter was its real founder and financial backer. She was a product of revival and edited a bimonthly magazine called the *Healer* which publicised all the countless and remarkable healings that took place. Here is one of the wonderful testimonies.

'Five miles away lived George Evison. His eyeballs (in which disease commenced at five) fell out, both of them, within a few weeks at about twenty. The poor, afflicted fellow was a curiosity. Hundreds gently placed their fingers in the empty eye sockets, little dreaming that they would thereby become later on witnesses to the "healing". Yet it was far more than a healing.

'Hearing of the meetings and having become a child of God during his affliction, he was conducted to the hall. After prayer and laying on of hands, a faint glimmer came. Within forty-eight hours, new eyes, perfectly complete, but about the size of those of a boy of five, had been created by the Creator in those empty sockets. A considerable number of the public, doctors, solicitors, and other well-known people gave written testimony to the facts. Through Mr Evison's subsequent testimony, more than fifty received faith and were healed of eye troubles or disease.'[76]

Diana Chapman continues: Bethshan was well-known, and it 'hosted in 1885 an International Conference on Holiness and Healing with 120 delegates including the radical Scottish healer James Alexander Dowie, who was later to found Zion

---

[75] http://en.wikipedia.org/wiki/William_Booth
[76] Diana Chapman, *Britain's Spiritual Inheritance*, pp. 107–108.

City, Chicago. This healing camp was a root of Polly and Smith Wigglesworth's healing ministry.[77]

Spiritual and physical healing manifests wherever the presence of God is, just as it was in Jesus' day. Miracles are a sign that God is at work in this or that movement.

Revivals and Awakenings

In 1904, thousands were converted in Wales through the Welsh revival and a third of Wales came to Christ. Joseph Jenkins of New Quay and Evan Roberts of Loughor were the main speakers used by the Holy Spirit to usher in a dramatic move of God which affected the population at large. Pubs were closed, and chapels sprouted everywhere. Even the pit ponies were affected because it was reported they were used to commands being sworn at them, but they were confused when they were asked politely!

The movement kept the churches of Wales filled for many years to come. Meanwhile, the Awakening swept the rest of Britain, Scandinavia, parts of Europe, North America, the mission fields of India and the Orient, Africa, and Latin America.

In 1907 and 1908, the Holy Spirit continued to fall in many places, such as in *Sunderland* where a mighty move of God began in September 1907. *A. A. Boddy* invited Norwegian T. B. Barratt to Sunderland. The result was explosive! Some have referenced this as the British Pentecostal Revival. It empowered people with spiritual gifts and tongues. Thereafter, Boddy held annual conventions until 1914, which were attended by all those destined to shake the world with their Pentecostal message. George Jeffries and Smith Wigglesworth received the power for evangelism and healing there, and Wigglesworth took it to the nations. His influence on American Pentecostalism in 1914, 1922, and 1927 was incredible.[78]

In 1910, the *first World Missionary Conference* was held in Edinburgh. (It was reported that no Catholic, Eastern Orthodox, Pentecostals, or black people were invited.)

---

[77] Diana Chapman, *Britain's Spiritual Inheritance*, p.108.

[78] http.//www.revival-library.org/pensketches/engpp_menu.php

It is interesting to note that just as white people went to Africa, India, and beyond; now it is the reverse – they are now coming here to re-evangelise us who have in part lost the fire of God's Spirit!

In 1906, in *Azusa Street*, Los Angeles, a mighty revival with extraordinary signs and miracles took place under the leadership of a one-eyed African American preacher, *William J. Seymour*. This revival also saw thousands of conversions and also exhibited speaking in tongues. Almost all *Pentecostal* denominations stem from these outpourings of God around 1906–1907, and the Pentecostal Church is reported to be the fastest growing Church today worldwide.[79]

World Wars erupt

Then came the two world wars, (1914–1918) and (1939–1945), the second of which alone claimed the lives of fifty-seven million people. Subsequent to these wars, our whole perspective of life changed; our world was turned upside down. Women were now doing men's jobs. Men lost some of their identity. Family break-up happened. Travel became easy, and people were scattered all over the globe; relationships fractured, and a deep loneliness led to increased depression. Technology took over, and this too often caused isolation from family unity. People lost their focus, belief in science all too often replaced religion – one man's truth became as good as another's. People were left floundering, not knowing what to believe, and some slid into anything that gave them relief: drugs, drink, promiscuity, fantasy, fatalism, or the occult.

Charismatic Renewal

But God was not asleep! He did not abandon his people! A wave of his Spirit swept the Western world. Britain, Europe, and America experienced this wave. They called it the *Charismatic Renewal* (1960s). Fundamental to this movement was a rediscovery of the use of spiritual gifts and the baptism of the Holy Spirit, thus

---

[79] en.wikipedia.org/wiki/Pentecostals#Background

mainstream Christians came into agreement with Pentecostals. It gave hope. It brought people back to God and gave them a sense of purpose. It renewed their faith and gave confidence that God was very much alive and was calling them to a renewed identity in Him. Where they responded, God renewed them from within. He built them up, and people came together responding to God's love across all denominations. They knew his voice and wanted to obey his every wish. They knew deep within them that he was the answer to all the problems around them, so their confidence in his power and love changed their hearts. When one meets someone on fire like this, one just knows without words that they have got what one needs or one turns tail and runs a mile!

Having quickly summarised how God has been working across the centuries, Diana Chapman puts it very beautifully:

'Thinking about the distinctive of these denominations, the truths they gathered round were precious and still are. I want to be among a people who embrace them all! I cherish the truths of the reformers, who sought to live a right relationship with God through faith and grace alone, with no performance necessary.

'Like all the post-reformation sects, such as the Baptists, I want to find warmth and fellowship among believers and be unafraid to take a stand for revealed truth. I want to be like the Friends, who valued the gold in all humanity and sought to be led by the Spirit. I want to experience "religion of the heart" like Wesley, where love and grace trump judgement.

'I also want to live on the radical edge of the "Prims" and, moreover, to have the understanding of the Brethren who understood that we are all priests before God. I want, like the Salvation Army, to love purity and war against sin wherever it is found. I want to experience the power of the Holy Spirit like the Pentecostals and value all the gifts of the Holy Spirit, including tongues.

'And I believe there is *still* more truth and light yet to break forth from God's Holy Word!'[80]

I completely agree with this. It is wonderful to see how great God's work has been throughout the ages and that we, in our time, can benefit from all the past learning and experience of our brothers and sisters who have lived before. There is unity between them and us, unity across time and denominations, and unity in the wonder of who God is who we all worship and who is inviting us deeper into His love.

Recently, I became more aware of what is happening in the Orthodox Church through the writings of Vassula Ryden,[81] who is being used by God to help us focus on God's way of uniting his Church. A prophecy was given that has gained momentum, which is very interesting. God showed a picture of the three strands of his Church: the Orthodox, the Catholic, and the Combined Protestant churches. God showed them as three rigid iron bars, but that He was in the process of transforming them into lit candles, each separate from the other. But it was His will to merge them finally into one candle, lit with his love that would shine forth strong and true to the world. In 2014, Pope Francis met Bartholemew I to pray together in the Holy Sepulchre. It is a real move forward, but it would seem we are still a long way from unity. Yet Jesus' prayer at the last Supper was, *'that they may be one as I, Father, and You are one'*.[82] To God, all things are possible. This is His world, and His will be accomplished in spite of us. Surely then, it is better to listen to His voice and keep our hearts supple in His love and our minds open and obedient to what He wants us to do. Jesus said, *'He who is not with Me is against Me.'*[83] This is our time, and it is our choice!

God asks us to pray. Some may think that their prayer is too tiny to make any difference and so lapse into prayerlessness. Let us remember that any beach is made up of tiny grains of sand. No

---

[80] Diana Chapman, *Britain's Spiritual Inheritance*, p.58.

[81] Vassula Ryden, *True Life in God*, www.tlig.org

[82] John 17: 11.

[83] Matthew 12: 30.

heartfelt prayer is ever lost. God collects them ready to pour out His amazing grace upon us. Then let us pray, as did our ancestors of old, that Britain would catch the fire of God's life and become lit with His light, His laughter (joy), and His love.

Perhaps this little poem could help us to pray in unity together. We really can make a difference!

We speak his Kingdom to come as it is in Heaven for that is His will. We speak His defeat of darkness, of death, of depression, and of dread.

With Jesus, we speak His Light, His Life, His Laughter, and His Love over our children, our homes, our families, our friends, and over our hospitals, doctors, and staff.

Light and Life and Laughter and Love over our farms, the factories, and mills; over the mines, laboratories, business, and shops; over our banks and trade.

Light and Life and Laughter and Love over our schools and all those who teach; over our churches, all pastors, and priests.

Light and Life and Laughter and Love over our internet, TV, and phones; over our transport, cars, ships, trains, and planes.

Light and Life and Laughter and Love over our prisons, our law courts and police; over all accidents and those who assist; over our government, parliament too; over our queen, her family, and staff; over the forces: air, land, and sea.

Light and Life and Laughter and Love over our country and God's wonderful world.

When we are together, standing in union with Jesus, we can change the atmosphere over our land through our thoughts, our spoken word, and faith-led prayers, for whatever we ask in union with God will be done. He has promised. So with confidence, we declare His Light, His Life, His Laughter, and His Love to rule and reign in our lives and our land.

CHAPTER 7

Unity with God and His Kingdom

God is the perfect testimony of unity. Though there are three persons – Father, Son, and Holy Spirit – in God, they work together in perfect harmony. All three always act together. There is never disagreement between them. They do not have separate egos (the part in us that needs to die) as we do, but They act in unison, in singleness of action. The essence of the Godhead is love, for as John says in 1 John 4: 8, *God is Love*. They never act separately. Scripture is very clear on this point. I was told as a child that God the Father created, Jesus the Christ redeemed, and the Holy Spirit sanctifies. So in my mind, I separated them. I even had difficulty at one time as to whom I was addressing in my prayers – sometimes Jesus, sometimes the Father, and then sometimes the Holy Spirit. They were somehow divided in my mind, but later, studying Scripture, I realised this is not the way it is. *They are one.* As Jesus said, *I tell you the truth: the Son can do nothing on his own; he does only what he sees his Father doing.* What the Father does, the Son also does.[84] And the Holy Spirit only speaks what Jesus tells Him. *However when the Spirit comes who reveals the*

---

[84] So Jesus answered them, I tell you the truth: the Son can do nothing on his own; he does only what he sees his Father doing. What the Father does, the Son also does (John 5: 19).

truth about God, He will lead you into all truth. He will not speak on His own authority, but He will speak of what He hears and will tell you of things to come. He will give Me glory because He will take what I say and tell it to you (John 16: 13–15).[85] They work in total harmony together, and Jesus is their perfect expression in human form,[86] and as Jesus is, so is God.

It is in studying and relating to Jesus that we come into relationship with the triune God through the Holy Spirit's revelation of Him within us. He teaches us to know God. We all need to be taught in this way, for it brings us into unity not only with God but also with each other. Unity with God is our aim. Not that we become gods, but that we are in total harmony with God. Perhaps the next diagram may be a help to see from where I am coming.

---

[85] The Helper, the Holy Spirit, whom the Father will send in my name, will teach you everything and make you remember all that I have told you (John 14: 26).

[86] He always had the nature of God, but he did not think that by force he should try to remain equal with God. Instead of this, of his own free will he gave up all he had, and took the nature of a servant. He became like a human being and appeared in human likeness. He was humble and walked the path of obedience all the way to death – his death on the cross (Phil. 2: 6–8).

Graphic 12 - The Relationship of Power to Authority

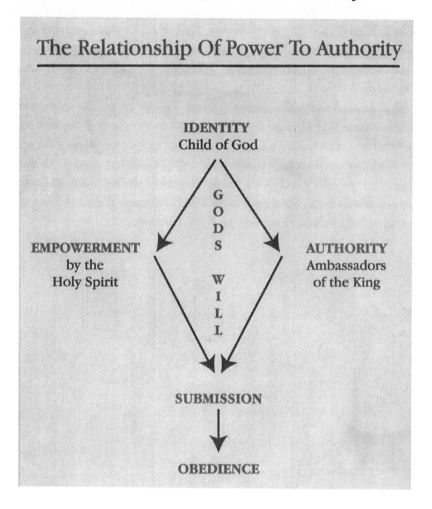

We are, in Christ, children of God.[87] That is our identity. Our purpose is to do God's will on earth, to bring about His reign and establish His Kingdom.[88] Our method, like Jesus our model, is to

---

[87] God's Spirit joins himself to our spirits to declare that we are God's children (Rom. 8: 16).

[88] This, then, is how you should pray: Our Father in heaven: May your holy name be honored; may your Kingdom come; may your will be done on earth as it is in heaven (Matt. 6: 9–10).

be in obedient submission to how He wants His will to be done.[89] When all that is flowing well, we are empowered by the Holy Spirit to be Christ's ambassadors on earth.[90] *It is not our performance but His presence within us that counts. It is being in union with Him so that His power flows out to those around us, often without our human input.* In Acts,[91] people would lay the sick along the path they knew Peter would be walking along. Without Peter doing anything but, because He carried the presence of almighty God, the sick were healed as his shadow fell upon them.

The power of God to heal and restore broken, hurting people flows through us as we are in union with God. Throughout history, this has been so, and it is so today.

As people spend time with God, so His presence emanates from them. As one stands in front of a fire, one gets warm! It is always His presence that heals, not the people. Does God want that for all Christians? Yes! I believe He does because Jesus said, *Go, then, to all peoples everywhere and make them my disciples: baptise them in the name of the Father, the Son, and the Holy Spirit, and teach them to obey everything I have commanded you. And I will be with you always, to the end of the age* (Matt. 28: 19–20). *Believers will be given the power to perform miracles: they will drive out demons in my name; they will speak in strange tongues; if they pick up snakes or drink any poison, they will not be harmed; they will place their hands on sick people, and these will get well* (Mark 16: 17–18).

---

[89] He went a little farther on, threw himself face downward on the ground, and prayed, 'My Father, if it is possible, take this cup of suffering from me! Yet not what I want, but what you want.' (Matt. 26: 39).

Be obedient to God, and do not allow your lives to be shaped by those desires you had when you were still ignorant. Instead, be holy in all that you do, just as God who called you is holy (1 Pet. 1: 14–15).

[90] Here we are, then, speaking for Christ, as though God himself were making his appeal through us. We plead on Christ's behalf: let God change you from enemies into his friends! (2 Cor. 5: 20)

[91] As a result of what the apostles were doing, sick people were carried out into the streets and placed on beds and mats so that at least Peter's shadow might fall on some of them as he passed by (Acts 5: 15).

The power flows from His presence. It is God who does this wonderful work of restoration. It happens when our presence is in total, loving union with His presence. Do we wait for this union to happen? No. We spend time with Him in the secret places of our hearts so as to bring our spirits in line with His holiness. Then, we simply do whatever He tells us to do, and He takes our water, and people receive His wine, as He did in Cana!

Obedience is a hard concept in today's world. Obedience is not an easy concept for those who have been brought up in broken homes, who have never had a father's loving guidance and who have had to make their own decisions at very early ages. This has become the normal pattern for their lives, for they do not know whom to trust nor to whom to be obedient. Yet in society, we do have to be obedient for things to work out. Take driving as an example. We have rules for how we are to drive to avoid accidents. It is good to obey the rules. If we go into the military, obedience is stressed, often in quite painful ways. No army can function unless obedience is a rule that is observed. When we give God permission to rule in our lives, when we join His great army of light, we need to relearn how to live our lives. That is why we need His rulebook, the New Testament first, and then the whole book!

Jesus, our commander, showed us, in His life here on earth, how to be obedient, both to His parents and to society.[92] Jesus paid His taxes! He always modelled obedience to His heavenly Father, for He never said or did anything from His own will, but only what He *saw the Father doing.* The bringing of our wills under the greater will of God is a daily learning process. All He wants is that we desire His will and ask Him to do it in our lives. He will do the rest. As He does, it becomes easier to hear His voice all the time and follow His lead. Then, we come to love listening and being obedient because we see that it works for us every time. At first, we need patience with ourselves, and we need to be accountable to someone in the Christian world who will help us grow. We need to

---

[92] And he asked them, 'Whose face and name are these?' 'The Emperor's,' they answered. So Jesus said to them, 'Well, then, pay to the Emperor what belongs to the Emperor, and pay to God what belongs to God.' (Matt. 22: 20–21)

study from Scripture how people heard and obeyed God's voice, and we need to learn what worked and what didn't.

It was through His loving obedience that Jesus has made it possible to bring God's Kingdom from heaven to earth. Yet not what I want, but what You want.[93] He went to the cross and paid the price, and God raised Him to life, to sit at the Father's right hand as Lord of heaven and earth. Even that which is under the earth must now obey Him, for He is Lord of lords and King of kings.[94] Through His perfect obedience, even to the cross, while on this earth, Jesus brought about a reversal of the consequences of our disobedience and ego-selfishness. He alone has the power and authority now. Satan and his evil angels must bow the knee to Him and so must we – they out of fear, and we out of love.

But we have a choice! Are we to be duped by satan and continue walking through life as though none of the above has anything to do with us? Do we continue to walk the walk we always have? Or do we live in the way God intended us to live in the Spirit, walking by faith, doing His will here below, getting to know Him more fully every day in our quiet times, and being obedient to His every wish? We start as His servants, but as we learn union with Him, we are raised to become sons and daughters, and this is when our wills merge with His and He can

---

[93] He went a little farther on, threw himself face downward on the ground, and prayed, 'My Father, if it is possible, take this cup of suffering from me! Yet not what I want, but what you want.' (Matt. 26: 39)

[94] 'They will fight against the Lamb; but the Lamb, together with his called, chosen, and faithful followers, will defeat them, because he is Lord of lords and King of kings.' (Rev. 17: 14)

And how very great is his power at work in us who believe. This power working in us is the same as the mighty strength which he used when he raised Christ from death and seated him at his right side in the heavenly world. Christ rules there above all heavenly rulers, authorities, powers, and lords; he has a title superior to all titles of authority in this world and in the next (Eph. 1: 19–21).

trust us. Then He says, *If you ask me for anything in my name, I will do it.*[95]

I believe God is stretching His Church right now. I believe He is preparing the end-time Church to be a glorious demonstration of His Kingdom here on earth. I believe He is drawing aside the veil between heaven and earth, to help us look up at what is available and not down at the circumstances in which we can so easily wallow. He is stretching us to expect far more than we have been accustomed to and to be more than we have felt comfortable being. He is looking for an end-time Church, powerful in His love, committed to His Son, and obedient to His Spirit.

Evil is escalating around us, and it will continue so to do, for the book of Revelation states this to be so. But at the same time, as God allows this to happen, *He is raising up an army, His end-time Church, unified in purpose, passionate about His Kingdom, and obedient to His every wish.* This Church unified, passionate, and obedient will stand victorious over the rising tide of evil that threatens to engulf the world. The world will have the same choice we had, to join the King in His Kingdom or get swept away in the evil around us. Seen in this light one might think, 'What kind of choice is that?' Obviously, we will not want to choose the evil. Like Eve, who chose the fruit, we have many times been similarly deceived into thinking we are choosing good when we are in fact choosing evil. Satan is the arch deceiver. He is relentless, and he never sleeps. Just as a wolf looks for the lonely sheep separated from the flock, so satan looks for the spiritual stragglers or those with no time for the secret place or for belonging to the Church. Our archenemy has had centuries of practice at deceiving human beings, and he is good at it. *Obedience to authority is essential to any army, and it is essential in the end-time Church. Jesus is the head, and we, His Body, all must be in unity with Him. This is the only way to see satan defeated and God's Kingdom come.*

---

[95] And I will do whatever you ask for in my name, so that the Father's glory will be shown through the Son. If you ask me for anything in my name, I will do it (John 14: 13–14).

So what is our attitude towards authority? Do we grouse and grumble under it? Do we resent it and tell everyone what we would do if we were in their place? Do we leave the ship because we do not like the captain? Scripture says that God appoints those in authority over us.[96] Sometimes, it is to mutually encourage us; sometimes, it is to bring to the surface things that need healing in us; *iron sharpens iron* (Prov. 27: 17). If we allow these things to be healed, we can grow and move on, but if we kick and squirm and hit back, we will live in this disharmony for perhaps all our lives or until we release it. Living under obedience is a powerful discipline. Jesus himself lived under obedience to His parents for thirty of His thirty-three years on earth. That is a powerful example to us. Scripture says, *Jesus grew both in body and in wisdom, gaining favour with God and people.*[97] He grew in the same way we can grow, by keeping in union with our heavenly Father and spreading love to all people around us, especially those in authority over us.

So what if those in authority over us are in error? God honours authority; He does not honour error. He often corrects it His way when He sees His children being faithful to honour the authority over them. We can bless, we can spread kindness, we can pray for help for them, and we can resist negative thinking and the urge to gossip about them. God will then honour our obedience, and we will wonder at His marvellous ways of doing this. He may remove us or them, or He may change both of us! God always uses the circumstances around us for our good if we let Him and don't take matters into our own hands to help Him out with our solutions! It never works that way!

There is no such thing as a perfect Church, a perfect pastor, a perfect Christian, or a perfect parent. All of us are flawed, but flaws show more clearly in those in authority. That is why Scripture asks us to pray for them specifically. If God raises you

---

[96] Obey your leaders and follow their orders. They watch over your souls without resting, since they must give to God an account of their service. If you obey them, they will do their work gladly; if not, they will do it with sadness, and that would be of no help to you (Heb. 13: 17).

[97] Jesus grew both in body and in wisdom, gaining favor with God and people (Luke 2: 52).

up in authority, how would you like people to treat you? Do the same to those over you. All Christians need to be accountable. No Christian is an authority on his or her own. The Pope's title is *Servant to the Servants of God*. All leaders need themselves to be under the umbrella of authority. The Apostles, even though working alone to spread God's Good News, came back to Jerusalem. Paul rebuked Peter when he was showing double-mindedness. There is a safeguard to our zeal and enthusiasm. It is authority, for God honours those who, like his Son, demonstrate obedience. Pride was the devil's downfall. Obedience to legitimate authority keeps us safe. No Christian should be out from under the umbrella of authority. When the rains come, and they will, without this umbrella, get drenched! Satan knows this, so he does all he can to sow discord, disharmony, and misunderstanding between the laity and the clergy, that is, between those in authority and those under it. He will even distort words spoken by a priest from the altar to his congregation so that they hear what the priest never said and stand in judgement of him.

I experienced this distortion once when I was listening to a ten-minute homily (sermonette) that a priest was giving. I suddenly became aware of something he clearly said that was contrary to what I saw as the truth of the Gospel. Anger started to escalate within me. How could he lead his people astray like this! Then he said something else equally not true to the Gospel message. I was horrified. Finally, it happened again. I heard three clearly contrary proclamations to how I understood the Gospel.

I was then so angry inside that I almost got up and walked out in disgust. However, I knew better than to act in reaction so I prayed for wisdom. I stayed until everyone had left the chapel, still waiting on God for what I should do. The priest came out alone to tidy up the altar, so I went up to him and said, 'Excuse me, Father, but did you say this and this and this?' By now my initial anger had subsided, and I spoke quietly.

'No,' he said, 'I did not, for that is not the truth. What you have heard are enemy lies. Sometimes, he can twist our words mid-air and cause real problems that way.'

I learnt a lot that day.

Let us all not just assume we are hearing correctly, but let us ask speakers to clarify for us rather than get into militant reaction at what we are certain they have said. Much mischief is spread in this way. The devil is cunning, and we must be one step ahead of him.[98]

Jesus told us to be aware of the signs of the times.[99] Let us take this seriously and be aware of what God is doing around the world and not just in our tiny part of His Church. We can get so preoccupied with our own version of Church that we miss what the Spirit is saying to *the* Church worldwide. Churches can get so busy with all that they feel they must do to keep everything going that they can even miss the Lord as He passes by or comes knocking at the door. The Church of Jesus' day did just that. The Pharisees and leaders of the Sanhedrin were the very people who missed His visitation. It was not the sinners or those who knew they were in need of help; it was those who were teaching others (so please pray for me!) and who thought they had got it altogether that missed all the opportunities God was giving them. I am so very grateful to Nicodemus, the rabbi who came to Jesus at night seeking truth. Jesus told him, and He tells us through this incident, that we must *be born again* (John 3: 3) if we are to even see what His Kingdom was all about. That incident has changed countless lives since then.

Humbly, we must all come to Him, who is the Truth. He, alone, can enlighten us with new revelation and dust away all the cobwebs and misconceptions we have inherited from the past or have met in our lives, for these keep us bound and separated from each other. This week someone from a Mennonite background came to me saying, 'All my life I have held resentment towards Catholics because I was taught that they persecuted us way back, and only this week, I found out that the incident I have held in my mind for so long was not done by Catholics at all but by Calvinists.'

---

[98] I am afraid that your minds will be corrupted and that you will abandon your full and pure devotion to Christ – in the same way that Eve was deceived by the snake's clever lies (2 Cor. 11: 3).

[99] You can predict the weather by looking at the sky, but you cannot interpret the signs concerning these times! (Matt. 16: 3b)

Catholics have persecuted Protestants, and Protestants have persecuted Catholics or other sections of the Church. We can carry these seeds of resentment and bitterness deep in our hearts, and satan can easily water them when we meet one another in the workplace. We are halfway into prejudice against that person before we ever try contacting them. We have historically damaged each other profoundly, and even the history books we are taught from are biased against each other. This keeps the resentments going from generation to generation. We have all been influenced by this. Isn't it time we stopped playing the devil's tune and started forgiving each other for past sins so as to come towards each other with openness and generosity?

Can you join me in praying the prayer below?

'Father, forgive us for excluding others, for yielding to the lies of prejudice, for spreading untruths about others, and for harbouring in our hearts resentment against other churches and other Christians. Forgive us for criticising those in authority over us and for not praying for them as You have asked us to do, whether in the workplace, the society, or our Church. Forgive us for preaching our opinions rather than what you have taught. Lord, dust away all prejudice from our hearts that keeps us separated from each other. Teach us, Lord, by Your Holy Spirit, to join appropriately together to worship You, in unity, as You deliver us all from our personal blindness and anti-love. Come, Holy Spirit, renew us all in the fire of Your love, and please revive Your Church.'

CHAPTER 8

Unity That Delights the Heart of God

Can you imagine how it must be for God looking down on the earth from His throne in heaven? What is He looking for as His eyes take in the whole scene? What thrills His heart most about what He sees? Why not ask Him to show you?

We are here to delight His heart. He is our heavenly Parent. Through our unity with His Son, we are His children. How does a child thrill your heart? Doesn't it give you a thrill of pleasure when a child puts its hand in yours and looks up at you with expectant, trusting eyes? Surely, it is that trust that brings out the best in you. *I believe it is the same for God. To delight His heart, we, His Church, need to put our hands into His and know, in the very depths of our being, that He will bring about His Kingdom (rule) here on earth no matter what the evil enemy throws against it.* We need to trust in His almighty power and stand together in His love, as a demonstration of His presence here on earth. *Prayer that is in accord with God's will is a delight to His heart.*

The one prayer He gave us is the secret to unity between us, and this is the prayer we were given to say together and live out in our lives. 'Teach us to pray,' His disciples said, for they had figured out through seeing Him go up to the hills so often to converse with God His Father, that this must be the source from which He drew

His strength and power. Then Jesus gave them His formula for unity, both with God and with one another.[100]

He said, *When you pray, say, 'Our' Father.* Jesus is recorded many times as referring to God as *His* Father: *I and the Father are one*,[101] *My Father is the gardener*,[102] *Father if it is possible, and Forgive them, Father!*[103] He has a deeply personal and unique relationship with His heavenly Father, and God is His Father in a special way. Our relationship is not the same, for all of us have had earthly fathers. Yet as Jesus is loved by the Father, so are we too when we are united to Him.[104] He tells us to pray corporately, *Our* Father.

---

[100] One day Jesus was praying in a certain place. When he had finished, one of his disciples said to him, 'Lord, teach us to pray, just as John taught his disciples.' Jesus said to them, 'When you pray, say this: Father: May your holy name be honored; may your Kingdom come. Give us day by day the food we need. Forgive us our sins, for we forgive everyone who does us wrong. And do not bring us to hard testing.' (Luke 11: 1–4)

This, then, is how you should pray: 'Our Father in heaven: May your holy name be honored; may your Kingdom come; may your will be done on earth as it is in heaven. Give us today the food we need. Forgive us the wrongs we have done, as we forgive the wrongs that others have done to us. Do not bring us to hard testing, but keep us safe from the Evil One' (Matt. 6: 9–13).

[101] Jesus answered, For a long time I have been with you all; yet you do not know me, Philip? Whoever has seen me has seen the Father. Why, then, do you say, Show us the Father Do you not believe, Philip, that I am in the Father and the Father is in me? The words that I have spoken to you, Jesus said to his disciples, do not come from me. The Father, who remains in me, does his own work (John 14: 9–10).

'The Father and I are one.' (John 10: 30)

[102] I am the real vine, and my Father is the gardener (John 15: 1).

[103] He went a little farther on, threw himself face downward on the ground, and prayed, 'My Father, if it is possible, take this cup of suffering from me! Yet not what I want, but what you want.' (Matt. 26: 39)

Jesus said, 'Forgive them, Father! They don't know what they are doing.' (Luke 23: 34)

[104] See how much the Father has loved us! His love is so great that we are called God's children – and so, in fact, we are. This is why the world does not know us: it has not known God (1 John 3: 1).

To me, this symbolises the unity that we are now offered, unity with Jesus and unity with each other. God is truly *our* Father, and we are all His children. Those opening words are so rich. As the Father and Jesus are one, now through Him, we are one too. It is this wonderful unity that enables us to boldly pray together to 'Our Father.' These two words are the essence of who we are individually and corporately. Together we are God's children, one great worldwide family, and we all have Elohim as our perfect parent. So let us look at this prayer together. It will unite us!

Our Father in heaven

Jesus brings our attention to heaven first and earth second. We are actually seated with Christ now in the heavens,[105] even though our feet are very much on earth. The Lord emphasises this point by making it the first sentence of prayer. It is as though He is saying, 'Keep your focus up not down. Know where you belong. Don't wallow in the pig troughs. Keep your focus on God, not on yourself. Get your priorities in line with God's agenda. Know where you belong.' Jesus has bought us with a great price, and we are no longer citizens of earth. We belong to God in heaven. Heaven is our home,[106] and earth is our temporary accommodation.

Hallowed (holy) is Your name, God

Have any of us even an inkling of an idea about how glorious God is? Throughout history, He has taken some to heaven to show them certain things that need to be spoken or shown on earth. He opened heaven for Stephen, the first martyr, to see some of His glory even as the killing stones rained down upon him by his persecutors. Today, I believe it will become more common for ordinary folk to be given this privilege of going to heaven as God

---

[105] In our union with Christ Jesus he raised us up with him to rule with him in the heavenly world (Eph. 2: 6).

[106] We, however, are citizens of heaven, and we eagerly wait for our Savior, the Lord Jesus Christ, to come from heaven (Phil. 3: 20).

seems to be removing the veil between heaven and earth. Our heavenly eyes are being opened, and He is revealing who He is in new ways, for His purposes to be fulfilled. He is a Holy God, perfect in every dimension, powerful beyond our wildest dreams. Elohim is love itself. Our God doesn't love as one of His many attributes. No! He *is love*.[107] God is a marvellous Trinity of love flowing between the Godhead in a never-ending stream, each sustaining each in a complete wholeness that never ends. God has no beginning and no end. As the angels bow in adoration around His throne, they catch a glimpse of something new, a new facet of God they had never seen before, and they cry out in wonder, *Holy, Holy, Holy* (Isa. 6: 3). This new revelation never diminishes, for there is always something they had not noticed before. Their cry of wonder is renewed all the time. It is perpetual. All angels and humans are created beings, while God is infinite, without limit, and He cannot be diminished. There is always a new revelation of Him for all eternity. To us this seems impossible because we are caught in a world that has a beginning and an end. God is so far beyond our comprehension that our tiny minds cannot conceive just how glorious He is. Our words cannot contain Him. Yet this God is truly our Father. It was Their Trinitarian choice to make us Their children. Wow!

This is who we are, God's own children, so no wonder Jesus brings us to that reality as our opening prayer. It is as though He is raising up our focus and saying to us, 'When you pray, remember who God has raised you to be. Come first to the courts of heaven and revel in My glory. Leave earth behind for a while and bask in My presence, for it will make all else come into balance and perspective. Relax in the wonder of who I am. Rejoice in Me, for you are My beloved child. You are unique and special, for this is how I made you to be. In My Son, I see you perfect, for He took your imperfection away and now I see you as I created you to be. So come into My arms and let me love you.'

No angel is invited in this way. *The intimate unity with God that we are offered is beyond our human understanding, yet His invitation for us*

---

[107] Whoever does not love does not know God, for God is love (1 John 4: 8).

to explore it is always open to us. So when you pray, Jesus is saying, 'Come to Us. Start your prayer from the right place. Come into the marvel that is God and pray from there.'

May your Kingdom come; may your will be done on earth as it is in heaven.

We are to speak the purposes of God into being. The verbs in the original text are verbs in the form of command. We are to command His Kingdom to come, and God's perfect will to be accomplished. Just as it is in heaven, we are to command it to be done on earth. That is why we are to come to heaven first, so from there we can proclaim His Kingdom to be done on earth. It is His vision that we are to speak into reality on earth. We are to bring about His purposes. As His children, we are to see the transformation of earth into His version of it, the one He created it to be. It is our privilege to do this. It is our role in His plan. We first need to come to heaven to Him to learn how we are to see this transformation established on earth. We are made for Him, we are created by Him, we have been redeemed through Him, and now we are to bring about His Kingdom on earth as it is in heaven. We cannot do this from an earthly perspective because our earthly eyes are dim, and we do not see as we ought. So we must start our prayer from heaven, seeing through His eyes what He needs to be done. We are to listen to His heart and come into His perfect will, for that is the only way anything good and lasting can happen. He has a plan, and we are His ambassadors to see this plan put into effect. This is how we are to pray.

Give us this day our daily bread (NKJ)

Ask, Jesus said, *and you will receive.*[108] We need the right bread to fulfil this heavenly purpose on earth. We are not just talking about enough food to eat today on earth. Jesus said, *But seek first the kingdom of God and His righteousness, and all these things shall be*

---

[108] Until now you have not asked for anything in my name; ask and you will receive, so that your happiness may be complete (John 16: 24).

added to you (NKJ).[109] And again, *Your Father already knows what you need before you ask Him.*[110] Surely, we are asking God for everything we need in order to bring about His vision in the tiny part of the world where He has placed us. He is not going to commission us to do His work and leave us destitute of the tools by which we are to do the job. These tools will vary greatly with differing circumstances. We are to pray what is needed into every situation, but it must not be just as we see in the natural; it must be as He has given us to see from His heavenly perspective. *We pray for the food we need for His will to be done.* Paul had learnt this truth, for he had learnt to be content, whether in prison, on a raging sea, in the midst of persecution or in the company of family or friends. In all these diverse circumstances, Paul had learnt to be at peace. However, Paul always knew he had everything he needed to do the job of bringing the Kingdom of God to those who knew nothing of it. That was his great passion, and he ran that particular race to the end of his life.[111]

Where are we with regard to Paul's mindset? Is this our passion too? *We need to contend with the opposition around us just like he did. God's Kingdom will not come easily here because there is much enemy opposition and we are not using the right tools which God has given us to see this victory happen.* We are to do the same as Paul, but in our own unique way, for this is a different time and stage of human development. The bread we ask for is everything we need to bring about the Kingdom here on earth. If we keep our focus on God's Kingdom and not our natural need, He will give us all we need. We can be sure of that, because He is our perfect heavenly Father. We need to trust in Him, for we have His promise that He will not leave us orphaned! However, as it was tough for Jesus, so it will be tough down here for us too. There will be opposition. Let us be

---

[109] Instead, be concerned above everything else with the Kingdom of God and with what he requires of you, and he will provide you with all these other things (Matt. 6: 33).

[110] Do not be like them. Your Father already knows what you need before you ask him (Matt. 6: 8).

[111] I have done my best in the race, I have run the full distance, and I have kept the faith (2 Tim. 4: 7).

content to trust in all situations. We can only do that if we keep our focus on Him, not on the circumstances. Lord, give us this day our daily bread! We delight His heart when we trust ourselves completely into His hands.

Forgive us our sins as we forgive those who sin against us

This is one of the most frightening sentences Jesus ever spoke, and He has put it in the form of our prayer to God. We are asking that as we choose to forgive others, You God, please forgive us in the same way. The measure that we give to them is the same measure that God will give to us. This is our prayer. This is what we ask Him to do to us. Wow! It can fall off our tongue so easily as we recite these well-known words. Yet how often do we truly realise what we have just said! Let us suppose someone is mean to us. They have said or done something that was meant to diminish us. Our most basic human instinct is to hit back or run away and hide, feeling unloved and undervalued. If we use our nature to react to what is said or done, then we will take this hurt into ourselves, together with all the other hurts we have received during our life. This can easily become a huge pool of pain within us, but we try to hide it away. We can even pretend to ourselves that it is not there, but it is! We have all been hurt in this way when we have acted in the natural, for it was the only way we knew how to act. From our earliest childhood, we have dealt with the damage other people have done to us in this way. We have learnt to defend ourselves against other people – how else could we have survived up to now?

But this tactic does not work when we are invited to join God's family. His Kingdom is not of this world.[112] It is not a natural Kingdom; it is a heavenly one. The principles governing it are totally different from those methods used in this world. Jesus came to show us this. He came to model a human life operating in heaven's way.

---

[112] Jesus said, My kingdom does not belong to this world; if my kingdom belonged to this world, my followers would fight to keep me from being handed over to the Jewish authorities. No, my kingdom does not belong here! (John 18: 36)

He has shown us, by how He lived, that fight or flight is not to be used to cope with hurts we receive. An *eye for an eye* and a *tooth for a tooth* do not work in the Kingdom of God. If we choose this way of acting, then He, too, will act to us in the same way, and He asked us to pray that He would! Wow! *So we are not to function in the natural, but we are to use heaven's tools to cope with this kind of pain.* We are spirit beings, not just natural ones, for we were created by a Spirit, God. Therefore, we must learn how to cope spiritually. So we look to Jesus for how to do this.

All His life, right up to His last breath, Jesus showed us God's way of dealing with those who hurt Him. He forgave them. He knew that they did not know what damage they were doing.[113] He knew they were acting out of their own hurt or natural pride. They were being satan's mouthpiece for promoting division, whereas Jesus came to bring us all together in God's love. Satan's way and God's way do not mix. They are as water and oil!

The solution to the problem of how we have always been acting is profound (i.e. in the natural). It is not a formula that says, 'I forgive you,' but leaves the whole pool of pain right where it has always been. It is much deeper than that. We are asked to allow God to change our whole mindset to the way Jesus acted.[114] We are asked to give all our natural self, lock, stock, and barrel to Him so that He can transform us, resurrecting the real spirit person within us and getting rid of our false self. The old must go that the new may live. The person who I defend is not the person God made me to be. I am defending a false image of myself – my natural self-image, my ego – but that is not who I really am. I am defending the wrong presentation of me. God made me beautiful in His own image, and that is who He sees me to be. In Christ I

---

[113] Jesus said, 'Forgive them, Father! They don't know what they are doing.' (Luke 23: 34)

[114] Do not conform yourselves to the standards of this world, but let God transform you inwardly by a complete change of your mind. Then you will be able to know the will of God – what is good and is pleasing to him and is perfect (Rom. 12: 2).

am a new creation.[115] That new person does not need defence. I do not need to attack someone else for now I am motivated to act as God does, namely in love.

This transformation happens in us every time we choose to act in God's way and refuse the enemy the right to add to our pool of pain inside. It happens every time we join with Christ and ask Him to meld our desire to forgive into His great prayer on the cross: *Forgive them, Father! They don't know what they are doing* (Luke 23: 34). Every time we join with Him in that prayer in the daily wounds that we sustain in life, we let go of our natural reactions and choose to function in our true selves. As we do that, our reservoir of pain drains out, and we realise that this way truly works. A mindset that may help us do this more easily is to separate the hurtful sin from the person through whom it is coming. The sin is one thing, and we can stand against it, but the person through whom satan is sending his stinging message is one of God's marvellous creations who has been deceived into sin. We need to pray God's mercy and grace for them.

And do not lead us into temptation (NKJ)

Jesus is the unity that we need to rest in every day. All of us are tempted. Temptation is an essential part of God's plan for us so that we may develop spiritual muscles. But we cannot stand against it in the natural using only our minds and wills. If we do, we will fail. We are using the wrong tools for the job! A helpful truth that has come to me recently is this. When I see someone doing something that jars and provokes me to reaction, instead of judging it in my natural mind, I stop and turn it around to a blessing. I see it as an opportunity to do real good to that person. Perhaps God allowed me to see and react so that I would turn

---

[115] So that it is no longer I who live, but it is Christ who lives in me. This life that I live now, I live by faith in the Son of God, who loved me and gave his life for me (Gal. 2: 20).

Now, however, we are free from the Law, because we died to that which once held us prisoners. No longer do we serve in the old way of a written law, but in the new way of the Spirit (Rom. 7: 6).

it around for them to receive the blessing God wanted them to have. If I stay in the natural reaction, I have deprived them of the blessing God had in store for them! Blessing is a powerful spiritual weapon because we unite our intentions with God's own desires, which are always to bless.

Last week, I was ministering to a husband and wife, both strong characters, very able people, and equally matched. They were at loggerheads, and good relationship was not possible. Their marriage was a World War III situation! Was the solution divorce? Neither wanted it, but to continue living in this way was destructive. What to do? *Both were functioning in the natural.* Both came to realise that they were defending themselves from each other because if they did not defend themselves, who would each be? A nothing, a wimp, a doormat. So the tug of war went on, and it was draining them both from functioning in their work. Even their health was showing the strain under which they were trying to live.

Christian couples will not have the healthy marriage God had in mind if they continue using natural tools. Much unnecessary pain will ensue this way. Our unity together is in Christ. *He is the one who unites us, and He is spirit, so our unity is a spiritual entity, and our tools are spiritual tools.* Our natural egos, that we are at such pains to defend, actually need to die! The natural person we used to be before we gave our lives to Christ is not who we are now. That person went under the waters of baptism and arose a brand-new creation.[116] So now we each live our lives in unity with the Lord and, as we do, we can live much more easily with other people, just like He did. If Christ is our unifying process, we will make consistent headway in this spiritual life to which we are called.[117]

Living as Christians, but using natural tools, just does not work! Satan has a field day! God is offering us a whole new way. Yielding ourselves to God in the everyday circumstances enables

---

[116] For when you were baptized, you were buried with Christ, and in baptism you were also raised with Christ through your faith in the active power of God, who raised him from death (Col. 2: 12).

[117] Anyone who is joined to Christ is a new being; the old is gone, the new has come (2 Cor. 5: 17).

112

us slowly to trust that He really is big enough to deal with our situation. We have to bring Him into the battleground of our lives and realise that people are not the problem. People are not our enemy. Our enemy is and always has been satan, who wants to kill, steal, and destroy us all.[118] When he gets us fighting each other, we are playing His tune and agreeing with his purpose. We need to stop defending the wrong self. Dwelling on our real God-given identity and praying for revelation of this for all of us, living in ever-increasing closeness to God, desiring good things for each other – this is what works.

But it is useful to have a battle plan when, yet again, Vesuvius erupts. Why not put up a red traffic light, mentally, in front of the escalating anger and stop defending the wrong self? Coming closer to God and giving Him the reins will stop our emotions from being enflamed by our minds.

Graphic 13 - Giving the Reins to Jesus

---

[118] The thief comes only in order to steal, kill, and destroy. I have come in order that you might have life – life in all its fullness (John 10: 10).

This works. I saw this work in the lives of the couple mentioned above. I had suggested to them that having a strategy to cling on to at such times is very helpful. We had agreed that this strategy would be the saying of this prayer that Jesus gave us, slowly, deliberately several times, thus consciously changing the direction of their minds and calming their rising emotions. They did this for one week, and it worked several times. It gave them hope for a better way! They used this prayer as a tool for unity, and they refused to continue to be divided. *Fighting satan together brings unity and stops us fighting each other!*

Whatever the temptation that assails us, let us declare this prayer seriously and concentrate on it, and satan will have to back off, for nothing evil can stand in the face of earnest, focused, and persistent prayer. When temptation is strong, unite and pray corporately. As this can happen individually, so too can it happen universally. Spiritual warfare cannot be fought using natural tools. When we come to the end of our own resources, we realise that our way just does not work. We are in a spiritual battle and must use spiritual tools. This prayer can be a wonderful spiritual weapon. It is not just a formula, but a mighty weapon against the enemy and a marvellous tool to bring about His kingdom of unity and peace.

Whatever our background denominationally, this is the prayer that all Christians can join in praying together. *This is a weapon we can all use to see the enemy defeated not just personally but corporately. It is a unity prayer binding all Christians together right across the face of the earth.* It is something we hold in common, because Jesus gave it to us.[119] It is a treasure chest full of His truth. It declares in just a few words the purposes of God and is a practical plan to see those purposes fulfilled. It is His strategy whereby His Kingdom can demolish satan's wicked hold over this world. This powerful prayer needs to deepen in us all the time. To pray this prayer slowly, sucking from each phrase the heavenly depths that are there, is an

---

[119] This, then, is how you should pray: Our Father in heaven: May your holy name be honored; may your Kingdom come; may your will be done on earth as it is in heaven (Matt. 6: 9–10).

endless source of wisdom and revelation. Jesus Himself instructed us to pray this prayer.

Deliver us from the evil one (NKJ)

It is falling into the deceiving temptation, whatever it may be, that leads us straight into the hands of evil. If we resist the temptation by God's grace, the enemy will flee from us.[120] Personal temptation is one way we all have to make our choice as to whom we are serving, but there are other ways satan can trap us.

We are all a part of a family or group, be it at work or play or be it a Church or political party. We can be led astray through those with whom we live. The blind can lead the blind, and they both fall into the ditch together. We can come to rely on these groups for our identity, and if so, they have become idols for us. If this happens, God in His great mercy will cause some incident to alert us to the danger we are in. Again, we have the choice either to face and realise the truth of our situation or to cling even more tightly to our idol for comfort and purpose. God has many ways to wake us up. He may use dreams or revelations, calamities or accidents, illnesses or tragedies to jolt us into His reality.

When I was in my twenties, I was training to be a nurse in England. Part of my duties at that time was to care for a man in his late forties who had had a major setback in his life. Healthy until that point, he had had a sudden coronary thrombosis. The treatment at that time was complete bed-rest. Suddenly, he, a healthy individual, was not allowed to do anything for himself. He had to lie absolutely flat and do nothing. To be suddenly in the hands of another person, especially one you do not know, is traumatic. One's body has stopped functioning in the usually accepted way. Life as one has known has suddenly stopped. One is now totally dependent on the hospital resources. It is a very humbling experience.

One day, as he lay there, he said to me, 'You know, this is probably the best thing that could have happened to me!' That got

---

[120] So then, submit yourselves to God. Resist the Devil, and he will run away from you (James 4: 7).

my attention, so I asked him to explain. This is what he said: 'I am a baker, and I am good at my work. I started with just one shop, but now I have five. I work hard every night to bake the bread and cakes for my shops, and I love my work. It keeps me very busy. I have a lovely family – a beautiful wife and two great kids. My job fits well into the family routine. I work at night while they sleep, and I am there in the morning to take them to school and to pick them up afterwards. While they are at school, I sleep. I have time to enjoy them before I tuck them up at night and then go off to work. We had it made or so I thought. We were doing well and had a nice house in a good area, enough money in the bank, and two good cars in the garage. I thought I was doing well. Then suddenly this happened. For the first time in my life, I have had to stop and think, for there is nothing else I can do lying here. I have suddenly realised that if I had gone on like this, I could have missed what real life is all about.'

'What do you mean?' I said.

He continued, 'Well, is life only about providing for my family? I don't think so. That is good, but it's not my real purpose in life. I have been asking myself some questions as I lie here, like why am I on this earth at all? What is life all about? What about God? I haven't given Him a thought for many years. Well! If He made me, and I believe He did, then He must have had a reason. There must be more to life than baking bread and having a family! Sister, this (referring to his temporary incapacity) is the best thing that ever happened to me. I have had time to get around to talking to God. If and when I leave this hospital, there are going to be major changes in my life.' He did leave hospital, and I never forgot that man. He had used what happened to him to get closer to God. God had given him a wake-up call! Would he just drift back into the old routine or would he really change his direction? I have always believed that he chose the latter.

Graphic 14 - Four Ways of Living

Soaring in the Spirit

Climbing to Self-Worth

Mount Reason

Humdrum City

Humdrum Existence

The Pit

This illustration shows four ways we can be living our lives. (1) We can be heading away from God, seeking all sorts of fulfilment that He has clearly told us will not fulfil us, and it will lead to death. (2) We can be climbing Mount Reason, trying to reach goals we think will fulfil us and make us people of worth. When we get to the top of the ladder, we realise that we are the same unfulfilled people as when we started. (3) We can, like my baker friend, think we have got our lives together, but God is not a part of it. (4) We can give ourselves into God's hands to fulfil in us the purpose He destined when He made us. *This is the only life that fulfils us, for it is the life for which we were made.* Satan is the arch deceiver, and he delights to see us struggling as we live our lives in the wrong way. This gives him much pleasure. Our whole way of life can be a deception. We are here to fulfil God's purpose for making us, not just to exist from day to day.

All the disciples were active in their own lifestyles when Jesus walked by and called them to follow Him. In response, they left everything and followed Him. In three short years, He trained them to instigate something that would eventually change the whole world. He formed them into a body, which He called His Church, and sent them out to take the Good News of God's love to all people everywhere. He calls us to do the same. We are here on a Divine mission. Jesus has promised to be with us on this mission and to protect His Church from evil, for even the gates of hell itself will not prevail against His Church.[121]

The Church, with Christ as its head, is the most dynamic force for good in this world. The Church, with us in the lead, is weak, ineffective, sleepy, and inconsequential. We can be deceived along the way. Satan's main focus is to divide and isolate the Church. If he can reduce it to sleepy ineffectiveness or galvanise it in the wrong direction so that we imagine that it is through human achievement and natural forcefulness that we will do something worthwhile for God, then satan may well be rubbing his hands in triumph. He did that once before, while Jesus died on the cross. He thought he had won, but he had blundered big time! For God raised His obedient Son to life, and now He rules and reigns over all. If satan thinks he has lulled the Church into spiritual complacency and if he has succeeded in deluding us to function in natural but spiritually ineffective ways, he had better watch out! It has always been when we are weak that God's strength is manifested best. God's purpose for His Church is about to be revealed in new and glorious ways. I hear the distant rumbling of the thunder of the Lord as He comes to deliver His Church from the evil we

---

[121] And so I tell you, Peter: you are a rock, and on this rock foundation I will build my church, and not even death will ever be able to overcome it (Matt. 16: 18).

have fallen into and to regenerate her into action that will finally vanquish evil from the face of the earth. God's purposes will be fulfilled, for He is God!

The Church of Christ

God, not us, will build His Church. His Church will be marked by unity under Christ, obedience to His Holy Spirit, and humble, loving service to all humankind. God will 'get our act together,' as illustrated in Chapter 2 of this book. He will raise up thousands of nameless, faceless people across the earth, who function in Him and are totally committed to His Son. Nothing will stand in the way of such a Church, for no evil weapon formed against us shall prosper.[122] Is this just pipe dream or wishful thinking? No! And again, no! Looking around at the state of the Church today, one can be tempted to doubt, but one remembers Pearl Harbor. The Japanese general who organised that attack is purported to have said, when congratulated by his peers, 'I think all we have done is to wake up a sleeping giant!'

God will have the final word. *It is actually the fallen divided state of the Christian world that gives me hope! When Jesus looked His weakest, God brought it into triumph, and He will do the same for us, His Church.* He will do this so that no man should boast, but that God will get the full deserved glory.[123] So let us look to God expectantly. As Psalm 24 says:

> *The world and all that is in it belong to the LORD; the earth and all who live on it are his. He built it on the deep waters beneath the earth and laid its foundations in the ocean depths. Who has the right to go up the Lord's hill? Who may enter his holy Temple? Those who are pure in act and in thought, who do*

---

[122] But no weapon will be able to hurt you; you will have an answer for all who accuse you. I will defend my servants and give them victory. The Lord has spoken (Isa. 54: 17).

[123] He did this to demonstrate for all time to come the extraordinary greatness of his grace in the love he showed us in Christ Jesus. For it is by God's grace that you have been saved through faith. It is not the result of your own efforts, but God's gift, so that no one can boast about it (Eph. 2: 7–9).

not worship idols or make false promises. The Lord will bless them and save them; God will declare them innocent. Such are the people who come to God, who come into the presence of the God of Jacob. Fling wide the gates, open the ancient doors, and the great king will come in. Who is this great king? He is the LORD, strong and mighty, the LORD, victorious in battle. Fling wide the gates, open the ancient doors, and the great king will come in. Who is this great king? The triumphant LORD – he is the great king![124]

I believe this prophetic psalm is for our day. All eyes need to be turned to Jesus, the Lord. We, His Church, must be prepared, for God is on the warpath. We can miss His purposes in these days by being so concerned with all we are doing that we miss His visitation. So let us submit to Him as He leads us and trust everything into His divine hands. Let us look up, for He is coming. We can be absolutely sure of that!

---

[124] Fling wide the gates, open the ancient doors, and the great king will come in. Who is this great king? He is the LORD, strong and mighty, the LORD, victorious in battle. Fling wide the gates, open the ancient doors, and the great king will come in. Who is this great king? The triumphant Lord – he is the great king! (Ps. 24: 7–10)

CHAPTER 9

Unity from the Beginning to the End

In the beginning of the world, God said, *Let there be light*, and light appeared (Gen. 1: 3). It was not the sun's brilliant light or the moon's gentle beam. It was a form of energy from which everything on earth has been created. Before this, there was only darkness.

Darkness and light are opposites. Where there is no light, darkness reigns. Once light appears, darkness must withdraw. We see this wonder happen every day. The sun sets, and night rules only to yield its throne again as the first rays of another day start dawning. It is beautiful to watch this cycle. From our earliest years, we understand that darkness will fade once light appears and that night will give way to a new day, which in turn will yield again to night when we can sleep.

Darkness and light in our lives

The same cycle operates at different levels in our lives. When the lights fail, we stumble around in the dark, probably hurting ourselves as we bump into obstacles. We are never more sympathetic to those who have lost their ability to see as when our electricity is suddenly cut off. Blind people are very vulnerable; they are easily hurt by those who can see. They learn quickly

121

whom to trust to truly guide them and who just does not have the time or the inclination. Yet again we see the same system at work as we grow and develop our understanding of the world in which we live. *Education is meant to enable our minds to let in light so that the darkness of ignorance can yield to the light of knowledge.* However, as with blind people, we can be hurt by wrong teaching, which can deeply influence our ability to see correctly. We can stumble around for years in prejudice, with warped notions that have been presented to us as truth in our early years. Galileo, for example, brought new light to the ways in which people had seen their world. They had been taught the world was flat, and he proved it to be round. Instead of being praised for this new revelation, he was persecuted by the Church authorities of his day, who were not prepared to let go of their ways of seeing. They had set themselves up as the guardians of sight, but they were blinded by their own self-importance and wrong judgement. They were not willing to let new light in. When we resist light in any form, we choose to walk in darkness.

God sent His light into the world so we could see. Jesus was born. The angels declared the wonder of what was happening to simple shepherds at night. *A great light shone around them.*

> *An angel of the Lord appeared to them, and the glory of the Lord shone over them. They were terribly afraid, but the angel said to them, 'Don't be afraid! I am here with good news for you, which will bring great joy to all the people. This very day in David's town your Saviour was born – Christ the Lord! And this is what will prove it to you: you will find a baby wrapped in cloths and lying in a manger.' Suddenly a great army of heaven's angels appeared with the angel, singing praises to God: 'Glory to God in the highest heaven, and peace on earth to those with whom he is pleased!' (Luke 2: 9–14).*

The shepherds responded by leaving their sheep and hurrying away to find what had been revealed to them. They were overjoyed to see the baby that was good news to all people.

Again, *it was the light shining in the darkness* that led the 'study-iers' of the stars to the humble crib in Bethlehem. *Where is the baby born to be the king of the Jews? We saw his star when it came up in the east, and we have come to worship him* (Matt. 2: 2).

Light produces reaction – and requires a choice (joy, that we now see, or blindness, to which we cling).

It was light shining in darkness that led both the humble and the wise to worship Jesus. What was the reaction of those in authority? Herod sought to kill the Babe, thinking to preserve his own throne. He sent his soldiers and massacred all baby boys in Bethlehem who were two years old or younger (Matt. 2: 16). This had been prophesied centuries before by Jeremiah. In this way, *what the prophet Jeremiah had said came true: a sound is heard in Ramah, the sound of bitter weeping. Rachel is crying for her children; she refuses to be comforted, for they are dead* (Matt. 2: 17–18; Jer. 31: 15). So Jesus came into the world at night when most of the world around was sleeping! And those in authority tried to kill Him. It was the same all His life long.

Evil is spiritual blindness

The spiritual darkness of evil is always in opposition to God's light. That is why Jesus, who claimed to be *the Light of the world*, came. The people of His day were blind to supernatural light, floundering around in darkness, not understanding what life was all about, but just living from day to day. So God sent His light into the world to light up the darkness, for He wanted to help people to see the truth of why He had made them and what their true purpose was. He wanted to open their eyes. Jesus was the good news that God sent. But would the people listen and respond like the shepherds and wise men or would they react in Herod's way? We know that many listened and responded, but those who were hardened in their own ways of seeing rejected God's gift, and in the end, they crucified Him. Darkness thought it had won, but light had come into the world, a light from God that could dismiss darkness wherever it shone. The dawn of a new day had broken night's power.

Is it the same choice today?

Yes, it is the same today, for we have the same ability to choose that the people of the New Testament had! Will we choose

God's version of life or will we continue in the darkness of our natural understanding? Natural man is ruled by reason, which is our highest natural gift, but there is more to life than that. *God is offering to raise us to His level.* God invites us to walk and talk with Him who is Spirit. *Will we accept His invitation?* Will we venture out from our small, comfortable world to meet Him?

We need to give up our darkness and see with His light. We need to change the glasses through which we see life to see it as God does. Creatures that love night hide away when dawn breaks and the sun rises. God's Son has risen in this world. Will we hide away or come into His light? Just as the shepherds reacted in fear of heaven's light, it is natural for that to be our first reaction too. Like the shepherds, it takes faith to leave *our sheep*, the things that hold our attention, and seek Jesus, God's gift to us. *Faith is a higher quality than reason*, for reason is of the mind, but faith is how our spirit functions. We are not walking minds. We are spirits walking for a while in a natural, thinking body. But unless we seek God's light revealed in Jesus, we will continue to choose far less than we can be. Living in faith together brings us to unity with Him; living in the natural can only bring disunity.

The greatest bargain of all time

We all like a bargain, yet here we are being offered the greatest bargain of all time, the free gift of eternal life with Love itself. Will we throw our chance away? If the local supermarket was giving food away free, wouldn't we phone our friends and tell them? So why not ask our friends to talk to God themselves and ask Him to give them grace to see Jesus as He is? They have nothing to lose except their own natural pride, arrogance, and fear. They have everything to gain. Jesus has said, *Come to Me*. If we will come, He will reveal the wonder of God's gift to us in a way that is meaningful to us personally. If we say, however tentatively, 'Jesus, I come to You. Please help me see,' then the whole marvellous process can start today. But for those who have already started along this road to real life, we need to come daily to Jesus, to live our lives closely with Him and allow Him to transform our darkness into His light.

Jesus' way or religion?

Jesus' way is unique. It is not religious, and in fact, religion can be one of the greatest stumbling blocks to seeing God's light. Religious people were the stumbling blocks in Jesus' day, and they were the instrument that pressured Rome to give them permission to crucify Jesus. Religion was full of man-made rules and was strong on performance. Yet when the *Light of the world*[125] came to walk amongst them, religious people resisted Him. It is so today. Religion keeps people out of God's way of freedom. If the Church of our day settles for religion, it will dry up and become sterile of real life. It will even exclude God as the Pharisees did, for it thinks that it is doing God's will. It will become blind. Blind leaders will lead people into their blindness, and they will all end up in the ditch![126]

So how do we know the degree of our present darkness that keeps us from His unity? We will know by humbly coming to the light. 'Show me God, please.' The Holy Spirit's job now is to lead us all into the Truth. If we are willing to be taught, the Spirit will teach us. The Spirit will lead us to Jesus, and Jesus will lead us to the Father.

The unity of God works together to lift us up from the ordinary, boring routine of existence we have called life, and it illumines the path to an increasing unity with God Himself. But will we go for it? *It is the greatest adventure*, this walk with God. God will transform us to new levels of His glory. Releasing ourselves to Him at all levels of our being happens slowly. It is a daily metamorphosis from the crawling grub to the wonder and beauty of God's butterfly. It is God's invitation to us to come up higher, to breathe His atmosphere, and to live His life with Him.

Letting go of all that holds us earthbound can be a challenge, for we cling to what we know. God respects our reluctance and never forces us, but as we let go of earthly attachments, He lifts

---

[125] Jesus spoke to the Pharisees again. 'I am the light of the world,' he said. 'Whoever follows me will have the light of life and will never walk in darkness.' (John 8: 12)

[126] 'Don't worry about them! They are blind leaders of the blind; and when one blind man leads another, both fall into a ditch.' (Matt. 15: 14)

us up to experience more than we dreamt possible. People can try to do this in the natural, so we get hooked on drugs, drink, sex, or anything that will give us a quick fix. Those things will only bind us further to earth, but the longing for more is deep inside us because it was put there by God. He wants us to stretch out to Him so that He can lift us up to His way of living. This is not a quick fix; it is for Eternity. As Paul prays, so can we:

> *I fall on my knees before the Father, from whom every family in heaven and on earth receives its true name. I ask God from the wealth of his glory to give you power through his Spirit to be strong in your inner selves, and I pray that Christ will make his home in your hearts through faith. I pray that you may have your roots and foundation in love, so that you, together with all God's people, may have the power to understand how broad and long, how high and deep, is Christ's love. Yes, may you come to know his love – although it can never be fully known – and so be completely filled with the very nature of God. To him who by means of his power working in us is able to do so much more than we can ever ask for, or even think of: to God be the glory in the church and in Christ Jesus for all time, forever and ever! Amen (Eph. 3: 14–21).*

Jesus is the only Way to life, and we need to meet Him personally *and join* Him in His great work of spreading God's message of love, standing with Him over enemy strategies. He is the Light of the world, and we can shine with His light together with Him. *The light of God is His love.*

For Yours is the Kingdom and the power and the glory forever. Amen. (NKJ)

God is Love. Love is not just a part, a process, and an attribute of God amongst all His other qualities. No! God *is* love. We will always know His kingdom, because it will evidence love. *Where people love each other and extend this loving acceptance to everyone around them excluding no one, there we will find the seeds of His Kingdom ready for watering.* His life is love. He gives this love as life-giving water to us to give to others.[127] *Come to me, all of you who are tired from carrying heavy loads, and I will give you rest.*[128] *When we can say the same, we are getting to look more like Our Lord.* As we come in our various ways to Him, as we agree that our old way has not worked too well, and as we let Him give us His teacher, the Holy Spirit, we each begin this transformation from self-centredness to love. Every day He teaches us through the circumstances that happen in our lives. If we have ears to hear, we will be guided into His way of loving people. His Kingdom is spread through love. *Unity and love cannot be separated.*

Love has many faces.

Love cares what happens to the unborn.

Love cares about what happens to the defenceless.

Love takes in the orphaned and tends to the needs of the aged.

Love demonstrates integrity in business.

Love demonstrates integrity in marriage.

Love gives to others and is able to receive from them.

Love is generous and does not judge or categorise people.

Love flows out to others and responds to them where they are at.

Love is in constant touch with its source, God.

Love is obedient to authority.

Love builds and enables others.

Love longs for unity.

Love is only negative to anti-love (sin).

Love is tender yet invincible. It is the strongest power on earth, for it is the power of heaven. The only way to bring heaven to earth is to live love here. As each one lives, spreading this love around, other lives are touched. Healing and unity are spread, and the Kingdom expands.

So how do we love in this way?

It is so simple: come to the God who is Love. Give him all that is in opposition to His love. Allow Him to show you what that

---

[127] Jesus answered, 'Those who drink this water will get thirsty again, but those who drink the water that I will give them will never be thirsty again. The water that I will give them will become in them a spring which will provide them with life-giving water and give them eternal life.' (John 4: 13–14)

[128] 'Come to me, all of you who are tired from carrying heavy loads, and I will give you rest.' (Matt. 11: 28)

means in your life. He sent Jesus so we would have a carbon copy of what His love down here looked like. Jesus took all anti-love into Himself as He died on the cross saying, *It is finished* (John 19: 30). So now there is no reason why we cannot live the life of love. It is our choice. The cross is a door to new life. We can walk through it, leaving all that we think we are at the foot of the cross. Naked we can walk through so that Jesus, who is waiting for us, can clothe us with his righteousness (right standing with God). Together we can then go to our Father God who is calling His children to Himself. *As we go individually through that cross, so we join with all others who have also made this vital step and share our commitment. We join the family of God.*

Graphic 15 - Going through the Cross

Would you join me in praying or would you prefer to put it in your own words?

'God, I want to love with Your love. Thank You for sending Jesus to take away my negativity to this love. Freely I give myself to Him, for I do not want to be ruled by sin ever again. Now fill me with Your love so I can give it away to everyone I meet. Help me to recognise all those who are giving this love and bring me into this great family of loving people worldwide. Teach me how to grow in love all the time. I trust you to do this. Thank you.'

Let us now worship Him because He will do what we have asked.

The Lord will lead us to those who can help us to grow. May we follow His lead, which is His voice inside us and the circumstances that happen to us. There will always be a deep peace inside that shows us which way to go. If the peace is not there, we need to wait and seek Him quietly until He gives us that inner peace. May we function in that peace, testing the waters with the thermometer of His love. Then we will know what is counterfeit and what is real. He will lead us, so let us follow His lead in confidence. His word is a constant against which we can test anything. Studying His word, learning about Him, and experiencing Him daily enable us to fall in love with Him over and over again. The more of Him we have, the more we want, until we become a message of His love. We become united with Him. In Him we share together His love.[129]

Am I suggesting that we leave our denominations?

No! I am suggesting that within those denominations, we change our attitudes to each other. We probably will never get all our theology into unity. Our minds try to understand the wonders of God. They cannot because our minds are finite and He is infinite. But let us not make our particular theology a god. Jesus is the centre of all truth, for He *is* the truth. Let us focus on

---

[129] Your life in Christ makes you strong, and his love comforts you. You have fellowship with the Spirit, and you have kindness and compassion for one another. I urge you, then, to make me completely happy by having the same thoughts, sharing the same love, and being one in soul and mind (Phil. 2: 1–2).

Him and allow Him to unite us under Him. Let us rejoice in Him together, in praise and worship. Let us bloom in His love where we are planted. Let us pray together for His Kingdom to come and His perfect will to be done here on earth as it is in heaven, and let us do whatever He tells us to do to bring about His unity and His love to those around us. People are not the problem; they never were. Evil is the problem, and we can stand against it with Christ, who has already conquered every evil through His cross. *He is calling us all to raise that cross and the victory it represents high over every manifestation of evil together*. His end-time army of love will see the glory of His victory happen in this world. Together, we stand with Him, for no evil formed against us shall prosper. He will deliver us from evil, for though it slays us, we will trust in Him.

All Christians agree that the Cross is at the centre of what we believe. Then let us focus, *not* on each other's peculiarities, but on what He has already made available to us all through that cross. When He said, 'It is finished', it was! The old way had been fulfilled by Him, and now a new day had dawned. The cross is the door out of this natural life and into life with Him. We can drop everything we are – good, bad, and indifferent – and walk through into His resurrected life. He will heal and replenish us and send us out together to those who have never heard what a wonderful God our Heavenly Father is. He will put us with those who have ears to hear, and He will give us the words to say, for His grace will enable us at all times to spread the Good News.

The Trinity of Love

When I was a nun, spending many hours in prayer, God drew me into the awesome wonder of the Trinity. It became a central focus in my spiritual life. I loved the uniqueness of Father, Son, and Holy Spirit, each expressing love to one another. I was enthralled by the endless flow of love between them that is their unity. The wonder of how the Trinity functions for eternity in this amazing flow of united love is a mystery. Could it be that God gave the world His Church to show forth His love here below? Could it be that we can demonstrate this Trinity of Love – the Orthodox and Catholic representing the Father, the many-facetted

Protestant Church representing the Son, and the ever-expanding Pentecostal Church demonstrating the Spirit? Are we meant to show forth to the world the wonder of God's Trinity? Could this be how God sees us all? Then let His Love flow between us. Let us love each other as never before. Let Him do His miracles of grace in our hearts that we may yet reflect the wonder of God on earth. *They* gave us *Their* glory. Jesus showed us *Their* love. The Spirit is bringing us into *Their* unity. The plan of God is truly awesome.

The end-time army of love

God is bringing His great plan to fulfilment. We are called to play our part in this great drama. Evil is escalating around us, but so is the great fountain of Love. It is rising worldwide through ordinary folk who are becoming passionate about spreading God's Kingdom of love wherever they go. Real love is irresistible because there is a deep desire for it in every human heart. It may start by being a desire for human love, so we may seek it in the wrong places, but when we come up against the real love, we will know it. We can resist or flow, but as we choose to flow, we get caught up in God's great drama of love, and there is nothing to match this. There will be an increasing hunger for love itself. There will be a passion greater than any other we have ever experienced. We will catch fire and become a spark and then a torch, from the great furnace of His divine heart, which is burning radiant love for all humankind. As these torches come together, a unity of love will sweep evil from the face of the earth. Evil cannot stand against the army of love. That is why we need unity. We need to let the Love of Jesus bind us together into this powerful driving force that dismisses all anti-love from its path. Is this a dream? Yes! *It is the dream of God.* Will we join God in this dream? Nothing will delight Our Father's heart as much as this. *Isn't that why we were made?*

Delighting the Father's heart means accepting His solution to evil, accepting Jesus, and putting ourselves completely in His hands so the Holy Spirit can bring us to our real destiny: unity with God.

Graphic 16 - Bird of Trust in Jesus' Hands

Can we trust Him to bring us into the unity he prayed in John 17, "Let them be one even as the Father and I are one?"

CHAPTER 10

Unity of Heart
between Jews and Christians

We have a problem in the very terminology we use. If we see ourselves as Christians, we who live in the New Covenant, and refer to our brothers in the Old Covenant as Jews, we have settled for a division which clutters our subsequent thinking into an *us* and *them*, whereas we are one family living our time in two different dimensions of God's revelation to us all. God made us all to have a close relationship with Him, and throughout history, He has expanded our understanding of this marvellous possibility slowly generation by generation. It has been a big learning curve for us all. Our Creator, the infinite God, has made us in His image so we can have a deep, personal, intimate relationship with Him, as Ephesians 3 says, 'That we may become bodies flooded by God Himself,' the infinite God and the finite human being in union. So let us not think of ourselves as separate, for we are one continuous revelation of God's presence with His people. To help us express that in this chapter, I will be referring to the Jews as Old Covenant believers (OC believers) and to us Christians as New Covenant believers (NC believers). Jesus, who was Jewish, stands as the central figure between the Old and New Covenants, for He completed the Old and brought in the New awareness of the depth of God's presence that has now been made possible for all humanity.

This chapter intends to show this gradual unfolding of God's revelation so as to dissolve any barriers that have arisen and bring us into greater unity of appreciation and love for each other.

Both OC and NC believers are God's special people called to show the world the Love of God. OC believers had a 2,000 year history with God prior to the birth of Jesus. We NC believers have also had a 2,000 year period in which to learn what unity with God's love means. Both have been learning how to relate to God. In many ways, the OC believers illustrate for us prophetically our own journey as we walk out of our own deserts into our promised land, as it says in 1 Corinthians 10: 11, *'Now these things happened to them as an example and were written for our instruction, upon whom the ends of the earth have come.'* Wouldn't it, therefore, be sensible to explore what and how they learned as revealed in the Old Testament? Yet many NC believers today, myself included, too often just concentrate on the New Testament rather than the Old.

So I found myself thinking that it was high time that I explored the Old Testament to see how God had prepared the people of the day for the coming of the Messiah and see what I could learn from them – and along my path came a very helpful book, which I recommend to you. The author Dr Michael Brown is a Messianic Jew, well versed in Jewish Scripture. He writes in a conversational style, which is a pleasure to read, and obviously has access to many Jewish authorities at his fingertips. The last few chapters especially concentrate on God's preparation of His people for the Messiah, and as I am well aware that in this chapter I cannot do the subject justice myself, I am basing much of it on Dr Brown's book, *The REAL Kosher Jesus*, with his permission.

I know I cannot complete this book on Unity without offering some thoughts about our unity as NC believers with our older brothers and sisters of the Old Covenant, the Jews.

So what is our honest attitude to the Jewish people? Is there any deep-seated prejudice lurking hidden in our hearts towards them? Years ago I went to a lecture given by the Rev. David Pawson. He spoke on how much we owe to our Jewish brethren.

It was an eye-opener, and I came away, as I am sure did many others, repentant for not endorsing and deeply respecting all that they have given to us Gentiles, in science, architecture, music, medicine, and many other aspects of life we take for granted. Can we say we love them and if not, why not? They went before us as God's chosen people and we are answerable to God for how we treat them!

What enemy lies have we imbibed that have set up barriers between us? Do we think it was the Jews that crucified Jesus? Do we, at the back of our minds, resent their rejection of Jesus as their Messiah? When the Lord means so much to us, do we have a real problem with how the Jews of Jesus' day treated Him? Have we ever bothered to explore how it was they came to reject Him? Do we even wonder if in our time we too could make the same mistake, caught as we are in the circumstances of our lives, and possibly not see what God is doing in *our* time? Let us explore together so that perhaps our attitudes can come more in alignment with God on this subject.

How had God prepared them? Why did they not see who Jesus was when He came? How came it they missed Him?

How did God encourage OC believers to see what His Messiah would be like?

1) God gave them leaders who were empowered to train them

Throughout their long history, He gave the Jewish people leaders who clearly evidenced the characteristics that His Messiah would have. Just to illustrate this let us take a few examples.

Abraham, the father figure of the Jewish nation, portrayed obedience to God, even to being prepared to sacrifice his son Isaac. And *Isaac*, in turn, showed this same obedience by allowing himself to be (almost) sacrificed.[130] How must Abraham have felt when God asked him to sacrifice his son. (I have often wondered

---

[130] Genesis 22: 1–19.

if he even told Sarah?) Isaac was their miracle child. Abraham was a hundred years old and Sarah well into her nineties before God honoured them with the promised son. He was obviously extra special to them, and then God asked Abraham to sacrifice him! Can you imagine what was going on in Abraham's mind? God had promised that through this miracle boy a great nation would be birthed that would bless all the nations of the world. It made no human sense at all to now ask that Abraham sacrifice him. Yet this great man of God obeyed to the letter. He had no idea that his act foreshadowed what Father God would later do and that Jesus, God's only Son, would die hanging on the wood of the cross, a sacrifice for the sin of the world.

Abraham is father to the whole family God was forming for all time.

Joseph is also a type of Christ. He was betrayed by his brothers, but later forgave and saved them.[131] Jesus was also betrayed, yet forgave and through Him all would be saved.

David, the king who was also a priest, clearly evidenced the Christ who was both king and priest. Psalm 110: 4 is addressed to David. 'Yahweh has sworn an oath which He will never retract. You are a priest forever according to the order of Melchizedek'[132] (an ancient priest of Salem, which was Jerusalem). David was a very human man who made many serious mistakes, yet he had a simple, humble, honest heart which God loved greatly. The future Messiah, both king and priest, would stress the importance of having hearts like David if we are to do God's will on earth.

2) God gave them many prophets

God gave His people many prophets, who each in turn prophesied concerning the future Messiah. Isaiah showed He would be a suffering servant, led like a lamb to the slaughter.[133] This we find quoted both in the Jewish Scriptures many times and also in the New Testament for Peter says, *'You should be aware*

---

[131] Genesis 42–46.
[132] Psalm 110: 4.
[133] Isaiah 53: 7.

that the ransom paid to free you from the worthless life which your fathers passed on to you did not consist of anything perishable like gold or silver; on the contrary, it was the costly bloody sacrificial death of the Messiah, as of a lamb without defect or spot' (1 Pet. 1: 18–19).

There were many prophecies concerning the Messiah, all of which Jesus fulfilled. Twenty-eight of them were fulfilled on the day of His crucifixion. It is revealing that as Jesus was dying, He focused our attention on *Psalm 22*. For this Psalm starts with *'My God, my God, why have You forsaken me?'* and it prophesies His painful death. But it also states that *'the whole earth from end to end will remember Yahweh and come back to Him, all the families of the nations will bow down before Him, for Yahweh reigns the ruler of nations.'* Psalm 22 ends with Jesus' last words *'It is finished'* (Amplified). Thus, the suffering servant and the King of Kings are linked together in this one Psalm.

3) God showed the Jewish nation He had special rules for the way He wanted them to live

The commandments God gave Moses[134] could not be lived in their entirety by human beings alone without God. God was enabling them to see that these commandments could only be achieved when God and man worked together. It was to be the very foundation of the relationship God was offering humankind, the glory of working together in unity. But the OC believers, coming from a slave mentality of 400 years, tried to obey these commandments in their natural strength and of course failed. The people learnt what sin was as they tried in vain to keep these rules of life.

So how was absolution and reinstatement to be given? Sacrifice was a common practice in all nations. They thought to please and appease their gods in this way. For the Jews it had been the custom from the times of Noah or even before with Cain and Abel offering up the best they had to God. It often involved the shedding of blood, the forfeiting of life, as the best gift they had. Now that the commandments were given, which they could

---

[134] Exodus 34: 1–24.

not fulfil by themselves, it became necessary for them to sacrifice to atone for sins committed. Thus, God planted in the whole Jewish nation an understanding that this would happen through an innocent victim giving his life freely to cancel the guilt of sin in God's eyes. The system of sacrifice became an integral part of their relationship with God. Their father Abraham had been willing in obedience to God's wish to even sacrifice his only son, and Isaac had agreed to be that victim. But God had stayed Abraham's hand. It was a prophecy of a future event, when God and his Son agreed to finally pay the price of human sin once and for all by the shedding of Jesus' blood. We can see that from where we stand in history, but at the time they could not.

In this way, God had planted in the Jewish nation an understanding of sin and how sin would be expedited: through an innocent victim giving His life freely. Jewish Scripture records this concept expressed many times. It was a concept they understood well. The commandments had been given them on Sinai to help them see that to live these commandments was impossible for humankind, so they would need absolution and reinstatement for the offender. They had this imbued into them, and so the system of sacrifice had become a profound part of their relationship with God.

Have you ever thought, 'How have the Jewish people coped with this after the destruction of their temple in AD 70 in which daily sacrifices were offered? There now is no temple, and therefore, no sacrifices can continue, so how do the Jews cope with this now? How are sins forgiven?' Some orthodox Jews are longing for the rebuilding of the temple so that sacrifices can continue. To others the whole concept of atonement became blurred. Some have found in their Scriptures the atoning power of the righteous. This idea sustained them through their long exiles, where many died. It was consoling to know that they did not die in vain, but that their sacrifice would be accepted by God to counterbalance the guilt of the nation. As Dr Brown (p. 150 of *The Real Kosher Jesus*) quoting, the eminent Rabbi Berel Wein writes, 'Would the Holy One, Blessed is He, dispense judgment without justice? But we may say that he whom God loves will be chastised. For since the day the Holy Temple was destroyed, the righteous are seized by death for the iniquities of the generations. So an orthodox rabbi who definitely does not believe in Jesus is telling us that according to Jewish Scripture and tradition the death of the righteous serves as atonement for the sins of other men.'[135] This understanding of atonement has been seen in Jewish writing for centuries, and even many of the lay folk are deeply aware of this truth. Even to this day, when a recognised leader or rabbi dies, the mourners will say, 'May his death atone!' The concept of atonement is deep in Jewish understanding. God was preparing His people for the great atonement Jesus would bring for all of humanity.

4) God gave them the weekly Sabbath and Seven Feasts each year to observe

Both of these were given in order to keep alive generation after generation the plan that God had for this earth and to help them recognize the Messiah when He came. He had created the world as beautiful and would bring it back to its original beauty. While He could have chosen to do that by a single wish, He chose rather to involve humankind that we would do it with Him. The Feasts were instituted by Him to be a constant reminder of the great plan of which they were part. The Spring Feasts, Passover, Unleavened Bread or First Fruits and the Feast of Weeks or Harvest were designed to point toward the Messiah, which we now know was fulfilled by Jesus in His first coming. The Autumn Feasts of Trumpets, Atonement and the Feast of Booths and the Gathering have yet to be fulfilled and may well herald the second coming of Jesus. Should you want to know more about the importance of the Jewish feasts, you may want to see my little video at this internet address: https://vimeo.com/user38965722.

So with all this preparation, why did the Jews of Jesus' day miss what God was doing? Why did they miss the Messiah?

---

[135] Berel Wein, *The Triumph of Survival: The Story of the Jews in the Modern Era 1650–1990.* Brooklyn: Shaar, 1990, 14.

The concept of two Messiahs

Jewish literature supports this concept, for there grew up among them the idea that there would be two Messiahs: one would be the suffering one who would expiate (make atonement for) Israel's sin and the other would be the ruling king who would deliver them from their enemies. They thought the first would come from the tribe of Levi from which all priests came, and the second Messiah would come from the tribe of Judah and be a descendant of King David. When Jesus came, the Jews were hoping for the second version of the Messiah, the one who would deliver them from the oppressive heel of Rome. After all, God had delivered them many times in their history from enemies. He had even brought them back from captivity several times. So it was natural that they were looking to God to break the power of the presence in their land of this Roman leader who thought himself to be a god! What an affront to a people imbued with the knowledge that there was only one God, Yahweh their God. The whole nation was crying out to be delivered, so they were focused on a Messiah who would be like David and would free them from Rome. *That is surely why they did not see what was happening in their midst.* They were focused on the wrong Messiah. They were looking at their need, that is, freedom from Rome, and praying that God would do things their way. But He had another agenda. How is it we can so easily miss what God is offering by insisting on our reality as our focus?

A good example, we surely could all learn from, happened in Nazareth at the very beginning of Jesus' ministry. He is in His own hometown, and He gets up to read from the Torah.[136] As he reads, there is an anointing from God on everyone there. He reads from Isaiah 61, that the Spirit of God is on him to set the captives free, give sight to the blind and set free all those who are oppressed. He sits down saying, 'Today these words have come true!' Luke 4 reports that everyone there was uplifted by God into a moment of divine revelation, for they were thrilled by His

---

[136] Luke 4: 14–22.

words, until, and it probably only took one person to voice it, 'Wait a minute. We know this man. He is Joseph, the carpenter's son!' And the whole moment changed from revelation to natural reality; the anointing was lost, and we are told Jesus could not do any miracles because of their unbelief.

Revelation must feed natural reality. It does not happen the other way round! How many times have we in our turn missed the anointing of God by insisting on being practical and choosing to live in natural reality? The leaders had heard of the miracles Jesus had done in other places, so obviously, this carpenter from Nazareth was someone special because no ordinary person could do the things He was doing, healing lepers, even raising dead people to life.[137] The authorities had to take notice because the people were following Him, and they naturally felt He could not be ignored. What an interesting question they asked Him, 'By what authority do you do these things?' Why did they ask that? Who were they thinking He might be?

Messiah or the expected prophet? Who is he?

God had planted firmly in His people's minds that the real Messiah would at least equal their greatest prophet Moses, who to them was so clearly from God, for he demonstrated this by his power to deliver them from bondage.[138] They had seen the Red Sea parted, and their way made safe to cross.[139] They had seen the whole army of Egypt drowned as the waters enveloped them. They had seen God give them water from a rock and manna and quails to feed them. (By the way have you ever wondered why they did not eat the flocks they brought out of Egypt and how did these flocks survive without grass? The animals were only used for sacrifice, and God enabled them to survive without grass.) The people had seen that their clothing and sandals did not wear out in the forty years in the desert. And all this happened through Moses who was their direct link with God. So their great Messiah

---

[137] John 11: 1–46.
[138] Deuteronomy 34: 10–12.
[139] Exodus 14–15.

must at least equal Moses in His ability to do miraculous things.[140] Thus, when they asked Jesus by what authority did He do these things, they were questing, 'Could he be our Messiah or is he the prophet we know will come? Is he the one God will be sending to deliver us from Rome? Could he be *the* prophet as great as our father Moses, for we know this prophet will come at the same time as our great Messiah, could this Jesus be he?'

We all know that one can be looking in one direction and then miss what is coming from another direction because we are focused one way only. God was doing things His way, but they were looking in another direction. We, in our time, could easily make the same mistake. They missed the time of their visitation and we could too, simply by focusing on how we want God to work and not seeing how He is working! Let's listen to the way we pray. Are we asking God to do things we want to be done or are we praying 'Thy Kingdom, come Thy will be done?' We need surely to watch the way we pray! God answers prayer, so let us pray in unity with Him and not voice our way of seeing how He should work! Let us keep our focus on what He is doing, or like the Jews of Jesus' time, we could miss our visitation. How valuable it is for us to learn from those who went before us!

Their error was to separate the roles the Messiah would portray, whereas God's Messiah fulfilled several roles in a single person, and through this one Messiah, God, in His own time, would show all that He proposed to accomplish. Jesus came 2,000 years ago as the suffering servant who would die taking the sin of all humankind on Himself, thus opening up for us all a way back to real relationship with God. Jesus also demonstrated that He had all power over nature, sickness, sin, and even death, for He rose from the dead triumphant. And Jesus will come again, but this time as King of the whole universe which he had created, and every knee will bow in acknowledgement of His Messiahship.[141] In this way, He would fulfil clearly the three roles of Prophet, Priest, and King. *Not two Messiahs, but one coming twice!*

---

[140] Deuteronomy 34: 10–12.
[141] Psalm 22: 28–29.

The Jews of Jesus' time wanted deliverance from the evils of Rome, whereas they were actually facilitating the greatest deliverance of all time without knowing it! God, through Jesus, was breaking the power of all evil that held the whole of humankind in bondage. God is so much greater than we are. As Jesus said on the cross, 'Father, forgive them for they know not what they do.'[142] How true that was. God was using even their blindness to bring about His divine purpose. Can we, NC believers, not see it this way? Isn't it wonderful to see how God even uses our errors to bring about His purposes? This is a very consoling thought. Surely then, we NC believers, who also act blindly ourselves and get things upside down so often, can come into union with our Jewish family, because we both share the poverty of our mutual ability to misunderstand what God is doing. Let us not criticise OC believers for getting it wrong. God does not want us judging each other. Rather, He is looking for humble, open, honest hearts (like David) dedicated to wanting His will to happen on earth . . . people who will obey His voice and do His bidding, like Abraham. But even when we get it wrong, that cannot derail His perfect plan from being accomplished. We are so much like the Jews of Jesus' day, so let us not stand in judgement over them. Let us rather rejoice together that this wonderful God whom we both serve will override our mistakes and even use them to accomplish His plan, for nothing can stop His great plan from happening.

We both are so obviously one chosen people, for the Old and New Covenants portray the same messages. God was calling them to live close to Him, and now in our turn, He invites us to live His life with Him. He will facilitate this in every one who responds to His invitation. When we do, we can see that He, through the Messiah Jesus, destroyed the works of the enemy and now has commissioned us to go and set the captives free, to open blind eyes and cause the lame to dance with joy.[143] Yet, where in today's Church are we actually doing that? Where are the miracles we

---

[142] Luke 23: 34.
[143] Mark 16: 20.

were commissioned by Jesus to do so that the world would know Him as their deliverer from evil? Our unbelief that His power can do that through us is what keeps the world in darkness. We still view the natural reality we see with our eyes, the fractured arm, or the tumorous lesion and do not know that we have within us the very presence of God to set people free. Unbelief crippled the Jews of Jesus' day, and it cripples us in our day too. God's presence is something we are all learning.

So how did God train the Jewish people to understand His presence with them?

We notice His wonderful provision for their every need as they laboured through the desert to the promised land. We read about the mighty battles they had to fight to take the land. We see that when they did things in obedience to God, they had victory, and when they did things on their own, they paid the price with heavy losses. *Independence from God is a recipe for disaster.* It was then, and it is now. How much of what goes on in today's churches is of our construction and how much is it us working together with God? It makes one stop and wonder. Faith, which is working with God, brings victory, independent thinking even when it is well intentioned brings defeat. God has always wanted a people who would work together with Him in every detail.

The story of David and Goliath[144] comes to mind. Simple, honest, confident David was used to living in God's presence and seeing Him defeat lions and bears, so why not this huge giant stood in front of him, blaspheming the God David knew so well? The Israelites saw the impossibility of them fighting this giant and were in fear. But this young shepherd boy saw that God was able to do it, so he chose a good stone and swung it well. How often in our lives do we settle for fear rather than do what God is telling us to do? Where is our faith in the God of the impossible?

The presence of God reveals His nature to us. What is God really like? We start questing because of what we see Him do, wanting to understand

---

[144] 1 Samuel 17: 1–54.

who God is in Himself. God wants us to find this out because He has revealed it slowly throughout history, first to the Jews and through them to us Gentiles.

How has God showed us what He is like?

God has been revealing who He is slowly, gradually stretching our human understanding to an ever fuller knowledge of Him. Way back in Genesis 1, God placed a clue when it said, '*We* decided to make man.'[145] But then, God focused for centuries on developing Abraham's family to gradually become the Jewish nation, surrounded as they were by many nations all of which were making their own gods to worship. God awoke Jewish understanding to know He was the only God of the universe. All other gods were false man-made entities, not real. The Jews were unlike any other nation in this profound belief that God was *one*.[146] Having reached that certainty of belief, God then enabled them to see slowly that God was able to be in two places at the same time. That was a real puzzle and stretched their concept of who God was. Even today it is still a stumbling block for some Jews. God opened their understanding in different ways.

The Shekinah Glory

God gave Moses, their revered leader, minute instructions so as to build God a house, a home for God on earth, so that He could travel with them. That was a big leap for them, for how could the God who was the one looking after His universe be at the same time in the Holy of Holies with them? They obeyed to the letter and made God's house, and His glory descended, and they knew He was with them in this mysterious way.[147] This was proved to them because when they sinned as a nation, God's awesome presence was withdrawn. When they came back to God sorrowing, they saw the glory returned. (In our day, the same

---

[145] Genesis 1: 26.
[146] Exodus 3: 1–22.
[147] Exodus 40: 34–38.

principle applies. When we sin we lose touch with God until our genuine repentance brings back His closeness to us.)

The Nebuchadnezzar story (Dan. 3: 24)

There are several incidents recorded in the Old Testament where God shows that He can appear as a man. I will just use this one story. Shadrach, Meshach, and Abednego would not bow down in worship to the statue of King Nebuchadnezzar and consequently were thrown into the fiery furnace which was stoked up especially high, yet they were not burned and were seen walking among the flames with another person. The king was summoned to observe this and said, 'There is one like the Son of God walking with them amidst the flames.'[148] I think God has fun when He uses a pagan king to speak His truth!

So could God manifest Himself in human form? Again, that was a big leap for OC believers to understand. Slowly but surely, they were being led forward to a new concept of God, one that He had laid the foundations for even in Genesis, the concept of '*we*'. Yet how could God be *one* and yet be plural? The Jews record this possibility by using *Elohim* as their plural name for God. Somehow then, God who was absolutely one was at the same time in some way plural. Perhaps we can see how God was opening up this understanding of plurality in God at the baptism of Jesus, where the wonder of the Trinity was first displayed in a practical way.[149] The Father spoke, 'This is My beloved Son in whom I am well pleased,' the Spirit descended as a dove and remained with Jesus, and Jesus, the Son, was being baptised. The Jews were being given evidence of what the '*we*' in Genesis represented, though they would not then have understood the dove resting on Jesus because at that time the Holy Spirit had not been given to man in the New Covenant way. That would come later. At this time, God was showing them the concept of Father and Son.

It was the beginning of a whole new revelation of who God is; the birthing of a new kind of relationship that God was offering to them now,

---

[148] Daniel 3: 25 (KJV).
[149] Matthew 3: 16–17.

the idea of which He had planted way back when he had given the miracle son to Sarah and Abraham. The wondrous gift He gave to His people now was the revelation that He, the mighty God, also had a Son in whom He was well pleased. What He had asked Abraham to do with his son was a prophecy of what He, God, was prepared to do with His own son, Jesus. We can see that from where we are standing in time, but it is small wonder the Jewish people did not comprehend what God was doing at the time. The Old Covenant was making way for the New Covenant understanding which Jesus would bring to humanity. To try to follow God's plan as He enables us little finite beings to grasp His divine intent is a wonderful learning curve and keeps us always at full stretch. We are looking back at these great events, but the Jewish people then were right in the middle of it and could only bring their current, present understanding to the situation. We must not judge them from our position 2,000 years later. That would be very unfair! To understand our brother Jews, we must walk in their sandals a while.

So we come to the burning question.

Why did they orchestrate and even applaud the crucifixion of Jesus?

From the Jewish leaders' perspective at the time, it seemed right. They were trying to keep Israel pure as they saw it. That was their sacred duty. There had been people claiming they were the Messiah before. To them, this man Jesus was blaspheming in claiming unity with God.[150] *Jehovah was one, so how could this man claim to be in a unity with God?* They did not have the grace to see beyond this then, so they rejected Him. Walking in their sandals we can understand this. The questions they asked Him were genuine questions. Yet we NC believers, looking backwards, have had a tendency to translate these questions as traps to catch Him out and could have judged their motivations somewhat unfairly. We, from our vantage point, can even use their misunderstanding as a weapon against them, but God used it for His divine purpose

---

[150] Mark 14: 62–63.

to be fulfilled. The Old Covenant was a preparation for the New one to be birthed. The Jews of Jesus' day stood at the crossroads between the two. From where they stood, they could not see the new thing God was doing. Their ceiling was to become our platform. The Old would give way to the New. God knew that the Jews of the day could not understand this and would actually enable this to happen.

They would reject Jesus, and through His crucifixion, He would set the whole world free from the bondage to evil. Then, through His resurrection, death would be conquered and the Holy Spirit be given to all who would receive what Jesus had done. Through His death, new life would be available. Winter would give way to spring. We, now in the New Covenant time, can see this, but they could not from where they stood. What an encouragement it is to see how God uses even our misunderstandings to bring forth His wondrous plan. Nothing will stop it happening! Little did the Jewish leaders think that even their act of real blindness, as they led the people into this awful tragedy of crucifixion, that God was at that time using their blindness to bring about the greatest victory the world has ever seen: the defeat of all evil through the loving obedience of an innocent son to His heavenly Father. God knew from their perspective, the Jews did not understand what He was doing, even the pagan centurion saw more clearly than they did, as he stated, 'Surely this was the Son of God!'[151]

Would it have happened if they had not orchestrated it? Now that is a big question! It had been prophesied many times and was embedded in their Torah, but they did not see that they were actually living in those prophecies; they were an active part of them. Did Jesus forgive them and does He forgive us when we get things completely wrong?[152] Yes. 'Father forgive them for they know not what they do.' Are we asked to enter into that same forgiveness? Yes. 'Forgive as Your Father forgives you, forgive

---

[151] Mark 15: 39.
[152] Luke 23: 34.

each other.'[153] So let this be our attitude to our Jewish brothers, for it is the attitude God would want us to have. Let us love one another as He has loved us all.

God was expanding the concept of His presence.

The Old had given way to the New. The New Testament was about to be written by Jews. They were the ones chosen by God to spread the Good News to all mankind.

Jesus came. He dwelt amongst us human beings. He showed us how to live close to God. He died, thus releasing humanity from everything that distanced them from God. Jesus rose from the tomb, now even death was defeated. The power of evil was broken; the cage doors had been opened. We are since able to live free if we choose to. Jesus was and is offering His abundant life to us.[154] He was and is inviting us into a closeness with God that was hitherto not even dreamt about. Having defeated evil, He then empowered His followers with His Holy Spirit and commanded them to go tell everyone what He had done so the whole world could be set free.[155] He manifested His presence and the sick got healed and demons fled and the joy of real life filled the air around His followers. Then He left and sent them the Dove, the Spirit of God, the third person of the wonderful Triune wonder that is God.[156] This Spirit was now to live within each person who recognised and took to their hearts what Jesus had done. The Shekinah glory now lives in human tabernacles (Holy of Holies). God lives in us and wants us to live every detail of our lives together with Him. We are not separate but are called to a marvellous unity. Jesus in us and we in Him by His Spirit for the great pleasure of Father God.[157] In this way, His Kingdom will take over this world. Through His followers living in unity with Him, the victory of Calvary will cover the earth, and evil, which

---

[153] Matthew 6: 7–15.
[154] John 10: 10.
[155] Acts 2: 1–21.
[156] Acts 2: 1–4.
[157] John 17: 11.

is absence of God, will be no more. God is love, and love conquers evil, for in the presence of God, it cannot exist.

The greater understanding of the unity we are offered

Jesus became our Emmanuel, God with us. That was the next stretch in people's understanding of this wonderful God. God wanted to live our lives with us, not us living our lives with God alongside. No! He wants to be involved totally with us. He wants an even greater presence to be true for us. He wants a deeper unity so that we live in Him and He in us at all times. He wants a living unity so our thoughts are His thoughts, and we react together to the circumstances that each day brings. We are to be one with Him (or should I say Them). John 17 clearly reveals that this is God's wish.

This was given us 2,000 years ago, but it takes a long time for us finite humans to get the message and then to live it. It is one thing to know the truth, it is another to live it, but it is available, and God is abundantly able to bring this unity about. Do we want it, or will we, in our turn choose our independence (our self-life)? If we do, we are the losers for that is the door to disunity with God, which is sin. Our choice is costly; will we trade our independence for His unity? We, NC believers, need to hear this loud and clear in this our day! We have lived 2,000 years of history to come, at last, to a fuller understanding of this marvellous part of the great plan of God which is unfolding bit by bit. Just like the Jews back in Jesus' time, we now in our time are just beginning to understand the wonder of who God is and what He is offering us. Perhaps this message of unity with God is what we need to grasp.

If God was not in a divine unity of relationships within the Godhead, God could not give us love and relationship because He would not have it to give. If God was only a single person, then He could not be the God of Love that we know He is (1 John 4: 7). Within the Godhead, there are three equal persons in unity. They never act separately; they are always in accord, for their unity is perfect. They are in a wondrous divine unity of love, and we are invited to join them in this wonder forever. Jesus showed this unity in human form by never acting independently, but always acting in unity with Father God by the power of the Holy Spirit.[158]

We are asked to yield our rational understanding and judgement, our independence of being, our separateness of identity, so as to enter into this unique unity with God. Only in God we can find out who we truly are and who He created us to be. God has revealed who He is in Christ. And Jesus is calling us to live in the Shekinah glory of His presence in us and then witness this to a hurting, pain-filled world. That is why we NC believers are here.

So what do today's Jews need to hear and make their own?

Dr Brown puts it this way on page 158 of his book, *The REAL Kosher Jesus:*

> *'Had not the Messiah taken our place, suffering on our behalf, we would have perished long ago. So the "Christian gospel" is actually Jewish, and the death of the truly righteous one – the Messiah, our great High Priest, the perfect sacrifice – atones. And this is not human sacrifice, an abhorrent practice condemned by God. This is our Righteous Messiah giving himself as a ransom for the entire human race, and, in the words of Isaiah the prophet, making himself "an offering for guilt" (Isa. 53: 10, ESV; Hebrew 'asham) – the guilt of all of us. This is a secret that must be shouted to the whole Jewish world.'*

Thank you, Dr Brown, well said. If today's Jews learn this truth, it will lead them into the New Covenant of the Kingdom of God. *Jesus evidenced God's Kingdom on earth. He showed what the Kingdom was at greater depth.*

We all have our role to play. For such a time as this, we were created. We are all called to work together so His Kingdom will be seen on earth. What a wonderful plan! What a privilege to be a part of this. How grateful we should be to each other, Jew and

---

[158] John 5: 19.

Gentile. We have both been called to carry God's light of truth, each for 2,000 years. Looking back on our efforts at carrying His truth, we have done no better than they did. But where would we have been if they had not carried God's torch prior to Jesus coming, He who washed the whole world clean? So let us be so grateful for the Jewish prophets and leaders of old. Let us learn from their stories, their examples of when they got it right and the way the whole nation battled on. Yes! They got it wrong sometimes, but they were continually being drawn back to God. Just like us! We should be so grateful and indebted to the Jews Peter, Paul, John, Matthew, Mark, and Luke the Greek without whom we would not have the New Testament. Where would we be without that? We needed them, and perhaps they now need us to, in our turn, carry God's truth and love to the waiting world. Each generation passes it to the next, and so it will be to the end of time. As yet, the veil is over Jewish eyes, and they cannot see, but the veil will fall, and one day they will all see and declare Jesus to be their Messiah. *Meanwhile, it is for us NC believers to carry His truth to the world, declaring Jesus the Jew to be both Prophet, Priest, and King; Creator, Redeemer, and Lord of God's wonderful world.*

There are many thousands of Jews in today's world who have seen the light and recognise that Jesus was indeed their longed for Messiah, but many more are still walking in darkness. This is just the same for us Christians. There are those who can see by the Holy Spirit the wonder of what God has provided for us: a whole new way to live. And there are many who cannot yet see this. Jesus gave us the command to love with His love. So surely this love needs to be given across the great divide between Jew and Gentile. We are to be known by our love. We are not here to censure and judge others but to pray that we all come into the light. The Jews, those who see as we do, and those who do not as yet, are to be seen as our brothers and sisters for we are all God's people. We NC believers need to respect our Jewish brothers and honour their 2,000-year carrying of the torch of God's truth, for we are a branch of the same tree grafted on to them by God. So as Pope Francis has recently been reported to have said to an Evangelical leader, 'Let us forgive one another and speak heart language to each other.' If we do, the mental barriers we have erected will start to crumble, as did the walls of Jericho long ago, and God will bring us into His kind of unity. So let us guard our tongues and renew our minds by cooperating with His wonderful Holy Spirit and allow God to bring us into unity with Him and with each other. We need all of us, from both Covenants, to give mercy, forgiveness, and love to each other just as He does to us all. His Love is the way forward.

However, it is the King Himself that will bring us into the kind of brotherly unity He desires. It says so very clearly in Ephesians chapter two (Eph. 2: 14–22), I quote:

> 'For Christ himself has brought us peace by making Jews and Gentiles one people. With his own body he broke down the wall that separated them and kept them enemies. He abolished the Jewish Law with its commandments and rules, in order to create out of the two races one new people in union with himself, in this way making peace. By his death on the cross Christ destroyed their enmity; by means of the cross he united both races into one body and brought them back to God. So Christ came and preached the Good News of peace to all – to you Gentiles, who were far away from God, and to the Jews, who were near to him. It is through Christ that all of us, Jews and Gentiles, are able to come in the one Spirit into the presence of the Father.
>
> 'So then, you Gentiles are not foreigners or strangers any longer; you are now citizens together with God's people and members of the family of God. You, too, are built upon the foundation laid by the apostles and prophets, the cornerstone being Christ Jesus himself. He is the one who holds the whole building together and makes it grow into a sacred temple dedicated to the Lord. In union with him you too are being built together with all the others into a place where God lives through his Spirit.'

I have covered a lot of ground in this chapter, so what has been my focus? I have tried to show how God has to date led both Jew and Gentile believers to know who God is and what the Triune God is offering us. In each generation both through the Old and New Covenants, God has developed these concepts and enabled

His people to understand little by little the marvel of the unity He wants us to have with 'Them' and with each other. It is a unity of love which is the very essence of God, and we are being called to share in this divine love for eternity. Jesus paid the price on Calvary for us to have it. Will we pay the price (our independent self-centred life,) to receive it? That is the question we have to answer, our lives will show what we have chosen. Lord, help us all to choose wisely. God says in Deuteronomy 30: 15–20,

> *'Today I am giving you a choice between good and evil, between life and death. And I call on heaven and earth to witness the choice you make.*

'Choose Life!'

I thought that this chapter was complete, but I was wrong, for a little while ago I attended a week's conference at which one of the guest speakers Peter Tsukahira, who has a ministry in Israel, spoke. He is living in Israel and has first-hand knowledge of what is happening there, and it is very exciting. He affirmed that many of the OC believers who have been living in Russia are now returning to Israel. This has never quite happened as it is happening today. Not only that, but as they return, the veil that has for so long been across their eyes preventing them from seeing that Yeshua was indeed their Messiah is lifting for many! They are rejoicing in the wonder of what that means for them. There is happening in our day, a unity between OC and NC believers that has never been seen before in these proportions. What a wonder God is doing in our midst! At last His Love is flowing between us, and it thrills my heart. Perhaps the return of the King is not so very far away . . . only God knows!

What does this mean for us?
What should we be learning?

1) It means surely that we must be aware of the mighty moves of God in our day and flow along with them. It is so easy

to bury ourselves in the immediate nitty-gritty of Church and family life and miss what God is doing globally.

2) Jesus gave us the parable of the ten virgins.[159] All knew their Lord; all were waiting eagerly for the Bridegroom to come, all were longing to enter with Him into the bridal feast. But only five did! Why? Five were convinced that He would come soon and had not taken enough oil for a longer wait. Only five of the ten entered. Perhaps this warning Jesus gave has real significance for us today. What is the oil we need in abundance? We are God's light to His world, but without His Holy Spirit oil, our lamps become ineffective for our light goes out. Only the Holy Spirit can keep the flame of His love burning strongly in us. We need great sensitivity to the Spirit of God in our day so as not to miss our time of visitation.

Peter Tsukahira pointed out the wonder which lies ahead of us, namely the coming reign of the King of Kings. As our OC brothers return as prophesied to their land, and as they acknowledge Yeshua as their Messiah, we are getting ever closer to the prophesied second coming when Jesus comes back as King of Kings, who triumphs over all evil and drives it away for ever from God's creation. All of this is in Scripture, in both the Old and New Testament. Thus all believers will be joined together, Jew and Gentile will be one in Christ for we are all God's family. Our ultimate unity is in the King of Kings.

Peter Tsukahira then gave me the contact details of a Messianic fellowship in Tiberias which I visited last year with my family. This opened my eyes still further as to what God is bringing about in our world.

Daniel Yahav teaches there an ever growing Messianic gathering, and on that Saturday he was speaking about the Feasts that God had instructed the Israelites of old to observe most solemnly each year.

Together with the command to keep one day a week sacred for worship, God designed seven feasts. In his presentation Daniel

---

[159] Matthew 25: 1–13.

gave an overview of the deep significance of these Feasts to us all. I had never seen this before, nor had I heard it mentioned in any Christian church I had attended. It quite excited me for I saw the timing of God in this visit.

The seven feasts God commanded Israel to keep without fail are divided into two separate halves. They include the Spring Feasts of Passover, Unleavened Bread or First Fruits, and the Feast of Weeks or Harvest. These feasts given 3500 years ago were fulfilled by God through the Death, Resurrection and Empowering at Pentecost (the beginning of Church). Then followed each year a long gap before the Autumn Feasts could be celebrated. Perhaps this gap represents the time between Jesus' life on earth and now. (We recall that it was 2000 years from Abraham to Jesus, and now 2000 years since Jesus). Could it be that we are about to see God fulfill the Autumn Feasts in our time? They are the Feast of Trumpets, the Atonement which is a time of suffering and repentance for the ways mankind has treated God, and the Feast of Booths which shows the wonderful covering that God has had over mankind, for otherwise we could well have destroyed ourselves by now. The final Feast is the Gathering of all God's friends from every age into one unity with Jesus as King and Head, and all evil finally banished from creation. These Feasts show clearly the great plan of God who will complete His plan with or without us. It is our choice.

(Should you want to know more, I would like to recommend you look at his teaching videos available on *www. penielfellowshipisrael.com*. It will reward you greatly as it has me.)

What started with the Jews was to be spread to us, Gentiles. God wants the whole world to be in His Kingdom. As of old, within His Kingdom, His law brings peace and joy, laughter and love, whereas outside there is weeping and gnashing of teeth. It is always our choice, the King's way or ours! This is so for the Church as well as the world! But as we come under His rule, obedient to His Spirit, we become lights to lead others into His Kingdom. Where the King is, the Kingdom will be manifesting and healing, deliverance and wholeness is increasingly happening all over the world. This is our time. For His Kingdom to be spread around us, let us open ourselves to God's Holy Spirit who alone can transform us from flickering candles to blazing torches carrying His love wherever we go.

Your Kingdom come, Your will be done,
On earth as it is in Heaven. Amen.

APPENDIX

Summary of the road we have travelled in the last chapter.

The first 2000 years.
(From Abraham to Jesus)

OC and NC believers are two parts of a whole people group. The family of God.

God's overall plan for His creation has/is being carefully worked out and we are all a part of it.

The Old Testament chronicles how God formed and guided His people Israel to realise in ever expanding ways who he was/is (a Unity which is also a Trinity of love) and His desire which was to live with His people, enjoying each other for ever.

He expanded their knowledge of Him through leaders (eg,Abraham, Moses, David) through Prophets (eg. Isaiah, Hosea and Ezekiel) and finally the Messiah Jesus.

He gave them rules for living (eg. 10 Commandments), 7 Feasts to observe pointing to the Messiah and His final rule on earth, and a physical presence , the Shekinah glory to go wherever they went.

Then He came in human form, as the Suffering Messiah, who opened man's way back to God; The Prophet and Priest and the Sacrifice who gave His own life for us all. He completed the Old Covenant and opened the way of the New Covenant to begin.

Summary of the road we have travelled in this book

The second 2000 years
(From Jesus to us)

Then follows the whole saga of life after the Resurrection of Jesus and the empowering and birthing of the church to our present day.

We covered in Chapter 6 a brief outline of how the Church expanded in Britain and how God, stage by stage, continued to teach His people about Himself and His plans.

The other chapters have examined in depth the importance of unity in order to see the fulfillment of God's overall plan. Without unity among one another we will not see His glory manifested here on earth.

God is calling us all to be in loving unity as he prepares to fulfill the Autumn Feasts, which usher in the culmination of His great plan.

Our unity of mind and heart shows His presence to the world, for it is His desire that none be lost and that all join Him in His Kingdom of Love.

SUGGESTIONS
TO EFFECT UNITY

1. God will bring us all into unity. Let us pray for this to happen His way and in His timing.
2. Get close to God to find out His heart for this time in history. Let us stand together resolutely for what is right.
3. Read about how other denominations think and try to understand them, looking for Christ in them until we find Him.
4. Be careful never to divide the Body (God's Church). So let us guard our tongues and clean up our thoughts so as not to think or speak negatively.
5. We could attend some inter-denominational Christian stadium meetings and mingle with others, praising God together to realise the breadth of His Church.
6. We can always learn from other Christians who are good examples of their denominations. Let us not listen to unworthy servants!
7. Resist all fear, putting God in charge of our life and often declare that this is so, encouraging ourselves and others.
8. Speak love, pray love, and join together in love with Jesus.
9. Obedience to the Holy Spirit is essential, so let us do joyfully whatever He asks of us. Being accountable to authority and blooming where He has planted us is usually the right way.

10. It is good to honour past heroes of the faith of all denominations.
11. Extend love to the whole family of God past and present.
12. We need to love God's wonderful world gratefully. As Pope Francis says in his latest encyclical, *Laudato Si'*, all human beings are called to look after this earth, so we need to come together into a unity of purpose to find better ways of doing this.

Therefore, let us keep close to God so He can direct us as to the part we are to play in His great plan.

Let us pray

Our Father in heaven:
May Your holy name be honoured;
may your Kingdom come;
may Your will be done on earth as it is in heaven.
Give us today the food we need.
Forgive us the wrongs we have done,
as we forgive the wrongs that others have done to us.
Do not bring us to hard testing,
but keep us safe from the Evil One.

For Yours is the Kingdom, the power and the glory
forever and ever, Amen.

Lightning Source UK Ltd.
Milton Keynes UK
UKOW02f1009250915

259245UK00002B/146/P